# REDIGGING THE WELLS

# REDIGGING

# THE WELLS

## Seeking Undenominational
## Christianity

### MONROE E. HAWLEY

Published by

**QUALITY PUBLICATIONS**

P. O. BOX 1060
ABILENE, TEXAS 79604

© Monroe E. Hawley  1976

Unless otherwise specified, scriptural quotations are from the Revised Standard Version Bible, and are used by permission.

ISBN:    0-89137-512-0,  paper
0-89137-513-9,  cloth

To Julia
My Wife and Co-worker in Christ

# PREFACE

There is a simplicity about apostolic Christianity that appeals to the common man. The most unenlightened person can appreciate the marvelous love of God in sending His son to die for us. Nor does one need a theologian to explain the golden rule. The American Restoration Movement of the last century was born of the conviction that the average individual can understand and apply for himself the simple message of the Master. The leaders of this effort to restore the primitive church called for all professed Christians to forsake their denominational bonds by returning to the non-sectarian Christianity of the early disciples. For the one trying to find his way out of the labyrinth of sectarianism this undenominational plea has a compelling attraction.

I gained a great appreciation of the principle of undenominational Christianity when I studied under J. N. Armstrong at Harding College. He etched the principles which he taught and by which he lived into the thinking of his students. The influence of great teachers cannot be measured. Truly, all of us are debtors to those thinkers of another generation who have pointed the way. There is much evidence to indicate an interplay of influence on this theme among those restoration leaders of the last part of the nineteenth century and the early twentieth.

For some years I have been concerned that we in the heritage of the Restoration Movement have to a large degree lost our appreciation of the undenominational plea. Some have frankly abandoned the idea as unworkable, while others give it lip service by failing to accept its implications. It is doubtful that the concept is as clearly understood among Christian leaders as it was at the turn of the century. There is a gap between our teaching and our practice. This is most apparent in the sectarian terminology which is frequently used, but is also evident in numerous other ways. The purpose of this book is to establish the principle of undenominational Christianity, to explore the practice gap among those seeking to be just Christians, and then to suggest ways in which our actions can be made to harmonize with our teaching. Probably no one will agree with all of the positions taken. Some will take sharp exception. But if the book prompts reexamination of the vital issues discussed, the effort that has gone into its writing will have been worthwhile.

**Redigging the Wells** is addressed to those in all segments of the Restoration Movement. It will probably have little interest for those for whom the denominational system is considered normative. But it is sincerely hoped that it will be of value to all who are the spiritual heirs of Barton W. Stone and the Campbells.

This is the first effort to trace the historical development of the undenominational principle in the Restoration Movement. It is also the first definitive treatment by one in the movement of the principle of undenominational Christianity itself. The only book of which I know designed to deal directly with the subject is G. C. Brewer's **Foundation Facts and Primary Principles**. This is mostly a collection of writings on the subject rather than being an exhaustive examination of the theme.

I am indebted to those who have made constructive criticisms of my manuscript, especially Edwin Broadus, Robert Lawrence, Roger Hawley, and my wife Julia. I wish to thank the Disciples of Christ Historical Society and Marvin D. Williams, chief librarian, for their wonderful cooperation in making available many of the periodicals and documents which I have researched. To all others who have in a variety of ways contributed to what I have written I express my profound thanks.

# TABLE OF CONTENTS

# FOREWORD

Since the general apostasy of the church in the immediate centuries following Pentecost, there has never been an idea more pure or more committed to either inspiration or the purity of the church than that which developed into the Restoration Movement.

So much contamination has been tossed into the historic stream of Christianity since it first poured from its original source, it is almost, if not altogether impossible to find the will of the Lord among today's religious orders.

Environmental pollution is slowly strangling our world. Unless heroic work is done and done now, contamination may destroy us. Likewise in the spiritual climate, pollution has almost blotted out the self-revealed God. Unless we can remove that pollution, the spiritual world may likewise suffer from the loss of a consciousness of God.

Constant renewal is necessary to offset the drifting course away from God. The wisdom of man, or even the interpretations of Scripture made by man, can never provide us with a clear picture of God's will. If it were possible for man to speak to God, there would never have been a need for God's revelation. The very existence of revelation precludes the fact that acceptability is found in human systems. It is up to us to go back and rediscover—every man for himself—the divine economy.

Only when men empty their minds of preconceived notions and receive with meekness the engrafted word are they able to realize the salvation of their souls.

When a spaceship is sent to the moon, or to one of the planets, someone has to be on guard constantly lest the spaceship veer from its course, miss its target, and wind up in oblivion. The church was launched on the day of Pentecost. Through the centuries that followed its trajectory changed as various influences were brought to bear upon it. It is necessary for us to check its course constantly lest the church miss its mark completely. If its trajectory is constantly corrected by honest application of scripture, it will succeed in the purpose for which it was planned. We do not feel that the church has any chance of succeeding in its purpose unless the restoration principle is carefully adhered to. To ignore that principle is to insure apostasy.

It is important that we recognize both what the Bible says and what it does not say. The church may lose its direction either to the right or the left. The authority of God in areas of silence is just as great as the authority of God in areas of articulation. We must not only speak where the Bible speaks, we must be silent where the Bible is silent.

—Reuel Lemmons

# REDIGGING THE WELLS

# CHAPTER I
# REDIGGING THE WELLS

"So Isaac departed from there, and encamped in the valley of Gerar and dwelt there. And Isaac dug again the wells of water which had been dug in the days of Abraham his father; for the Philistines had stopped them after the death of Abraham; and he gave them the names which his father had given them" (Genesis 26:17,18).

Isaac called the well "Rehoboth" because the herdsmen of Gerar had at last given him "room." Twice before he had redug his father's wells, only to have their possession contested by the enemy. Now, having removed the debris from a well near Beersheba, he was able to quaff the pure water drawn from the soil of the barren Negeb. The water that had sustained Abraham and his flocks now supported him. The earth and the rubble that had made it inaccessible for so long were now removed, revealing a fountain of life-giving water.

Jesus beckons his disciples to drink deeply of the Wells of living water which he provides. "If any one thirst, let him come to me and drink. He who believes in me, as the scripture has said, 'Out of his heart shall flow rivers of living water'" (John 7:37, 38). As the ultimate Source, he is "the way, and the truth, and the life" (John 14:6). He declares, "And you will know the truth, and the truth will make you free" (John 8:32).

Unfortunately, we live in an age in which the truth is difficult to find, not because of its unavailability, but because the confusion of a sectarian world has bewildered the minds of the truth seekers. Out of three hundred separate denominational voices, how can one who would be freed from the shackles of sin find that living water which Jesus told the woman at Jacob's well would cause one never again to thirst? (John 4:13,14).

The evils of a sectarian religious world are evident upon cursory investigation. To begin with, the followers of Jesus are badly divided. A few hours before His betrayal the Master entreated the Father, "I do not pray for these only, but also for those who believe in me through their word, that they may all be one; even as thou, Father, art in me, and I in thee, that they also may be one in us, so that the world may believe that thou hast sent me" (John 17:20,21). This petition has not been fulfilled in our generation and the current denominational system has contributed to the failure. No thinking man can honestly defend the divisiveness of our age as being pleasing to God.

The division ensuing from sectarianism is also a major deterrent to those who are honestly searching for the Way. Consider the plight of the man who, realizing his deep need, determines to follow Jesus. He knows but little of the Bible and is even unaware of how to go about studying the Holy Word. He decides to visit the denominations of his community in the hope of discovering one that meets his needs. He inquires of the teaching of each group. Some inform him, "We're all going to the same place, just traveling different roads." He soon realizes that the conflicting information he receives belies this theory. All these roads cannot be right since they point in different directions. The more he asks, the more confused he becomes. Finally, overwhelmed with discouragement at the prospect of really finding Jesus, he gives up, another victim of sectarianism.

It is also apparent that denominationalism inevitably perverts the pattern of the gospel of Christ. Truth is not contradictory. In mathematics two plus three cannot equal both five and six at the same time. Both answers could be wrong, but certainly no more than one is correct. Similarly, when several opposing responses are given to the same religious question, presuming that words are adequately defined, no more than one can be correct. All others must be at least partially in error. The current system, as will be shown, must share the blame for this condition. Only when God's people are one will unity in doctrine be possible.

It is probable that to the average person there is slight difference between the words **denomination** and **sect**. Dictionaries identify them as synonyms. If there is a difference in the popular mind it is that sectarianism is more likely than denominationalism to be equated with factionalism. **Denomination** signifies a name or designation and when used in the religious sense denotes a religious body. **Sect** also applies to such an organization, but it can also mean a dissenting or schismatic group. The Greek word **hairesis,** translated sect in the New Testament, literally means the act of taking or capturing, but religiously denotes a party that has separated itself from others. It is from this word that our English word **heresy** is derived.

Special definitions are given by sociologists to **sect** and **denomination.** As so used they have different meanings. The sociological viewpoint will be discussed in another chapter, but since relatively few people, other than sociologists and religious historians, are even aware of these distinctive meanings, they will not otherwise be considered. For the sake of simplification, and perhaps over-simplification, the popular definitions will be followed and **sect** and **denomination** will be used interchangeably. Likewise, **sectarianism** and **denominationalism** will be considered the same spiritual malady.

How did the debris of sectarianism come to fill the well of living water? As one digs through layer upon layer of history he discovers that a multitude of religious denominations have sprung from the sixteenth century Protestant Reformation. There were four chief fountain-heads of this effort: (1) the Lutheran movement begun by Martin Luther from which have emerged the various Lutheran churches; (2) the Reformed movement begun by Ulrich Zwingli and carried on by John Calvin from which have originated such Reformed churches as the Presbyterian; (3) the Anglican effort of King Henry VIII of England which produced the Church of England and the Episcopal Church; and (4) the various Anabaptist movements, widely diverse in nature, from which have come such groups as the Mennonites.

With few exceptions each denomination began as an effort to reform existing religious bodies. Luther sought to recover the biblical doctrine of justification by faith, largely forgotten by the Roman Catholic Church of which he was a priest. The Baptists sought a return to the apostolic practice of immersion, while the Methodists, led by John Wesley, endeavored to put greater fervor into the Church of England of which they were originally a part. Unfortunately, the reformers of the sixteenth and seventeenth centuries did not all begin at the same point. Because they sought to reform a corrupt condition rather than to restore the

17

original, a Pandora's box of confusion resulted. What was needed was a return to the model of the early church. Reformation results in a patchwork structure, while restoration, if correctly followed, builds from the blueprints and reconstructs the original.

When one digs down beyond the Protestant Reformation he still does not discover a unified church. While the number of denominations in the middle ages is not so great, he finds two major Catholic bodies plus several smaller sects. The Catholic Church, after years of internal strife, finally divided in 1054 into the Roman and Orthodox parties when the Roman legates, on behalf of the Roman pope, laid a bull of excommunication against the patriarch of Constantinople on the high altar of the Church of Sophia.

Even prior to 1054 it is generally agreed that the body which professes to trace itself back to the apostles bore little resemblance to the first century church of which we read in the New Testament. In the intervening centuries an apostasy from primitive Christianity had taken place. The congregational government of the early church was replaced by a hierarchy. Multitudes of doctrinal deviations from the teachings of Jesus and His apostles were introduced. As early as the second century the departure from the apostolic moorings is apparent. Paul had earlier warned the elders at Ephesus of an impending apostasy when he declared, "I know that after my departure fierce wolves will come in among you, not sparing the flock; and from among your own selves will arise men speaking perverse things, to draw away the disciples after them" (Acts 20:29, 30).

Only when the rubble of the centuries is finally removed and we reach the church guided by the apostles do we find the pure Christianity for which we seek. The Protestant Reformation, which is responsible for the multiplicity of existing bodies, was a sincere effort to reform the accumulated corruptions introduced into the Christian faith through the centuries.

Let us, then, seek to rediscover the church as it was known to those living in apostolic days. The necessity of such a reexamination is apparent when we consider that it has always been the tendency of man to depart from God. Such departures are generally so slow that those involved in them cannot realize at the time that they are occurring. It is only when one compares current teaching and practices with the original that the changes become apparent. Even within a restoration effort it is constantly necessary to reassess our positions in light of the model lest we restore the restoration rather than the original church. Restoration, to be effective, must be a continuing process.

The term **church** is a somewhat unfortunate translation of the Greek **ekklesia**. While our English word is derived from an expression meaning "belonging to the Lord," **ekklesia** originally designated a "called out" body of people, an assembly convened at a public place for deliberation. The New England town meeting expresses the idea. There is some question as to whether the "called out" idea inheres in the New Testament use of **ekklesia** as applied to the body of disciples of Jesus. Be that as it may, the early church is portrayed in the scriptures as a called out people. Peter speaks of the Christian's "call and election" (2 Peter 1:10) and enlarges on the concept by declaring, "But you are a chosen race, a royal priesthood, a holy nation, God's own people, that you may declare the wonderful deeds of him who **called you out of darkness into his marvelous light. Once you were no people but now you are God's people;** once you had not received mercy but now you have received mercy" (1 Peter 2:9,10). The basic idea of the **ekklesia,** then, is that it is the people of the Lord, called by the gospel from the darkness of the world into the light of God.

There are various senses in which the **ekklesia** (or **church** as we shall hereafter speak of it) is used. It often denotes the universal body of Christ. In this sense Jesus declares, "On this rock I will build my church" (Matthew 16:18). It is of all of Christ's disciples that Paul affirms, "And he has put all things under his feet and has made him the head over all things for the church, which is his body, the fulness of him who fills all in all" (Ephesians 1:22,23). Again, "He is the head of the body, the church" (Colossians 1:18). There are many instances of this usage.

On other occasions the term indicates the local congregation. Thus we read that "News of this came to the ears of the church in Jerusalem" (Acts 11:22), and Paul "called to him the elders of the church" (Acts 20:17).

Occasionally the word designates the actual assembly of the saints as when Paul writes, "When you assemble as a church, I hear that there are divisions among you" (1 Corinthians 11:18). (See also 1 Corinthians 14:19, 28, 35). It may also refer to a company of Christians belonging to one's family or, perhaps, those who customarily assemble in a given home. Thus Paul writes the Corinthians, "Aquila and Prisca, together with the church in their house, send you hearty greetings in the Lord" (1 Corinthians 16:19). In the plural the word may suggest congregations in a state or province as when Paul addresses "the churches of Galatia" (Galatians 1:2), or when John writes "to the seven churches that are in Asia" (Revelation 1:4). Observe that the word as used in the New Testament never designates the place of worship.

In this book we are concerned primarily with the word **church** in the universal sense, and secondarily, with the local congregations of the divine body. If we can clearly understand the biblical meaning of the **ekklesia** of God, we will have gone far in comprehending the message of this book: **Undenominational Christianity**.

The first use of **church** in the Acts of the Apostles is soon after the body of Christ was established on the day of Pentecost. "And the Lord added to the church daily such as should be saved" (Acts 2:47—King James Version). "And the Lord added to their number day by day those who were being saved" (Revised Standard Version). Since most manuscript evidence does not support it, the majority of versions do not use **church** in the verse. However, those referred to were added to something, and few would be disposed to deny that it is the church that Luke had in mind.

It is important to note that those who are added to the church are the saved. Biblically speaking, the church is the saved. If one has been redeemed from his sins, he is thereby added by the Lord to His church. The identity between the saved and the church is well expressed in this statement:

"The church Christ built includes all the saved; and it includes no one else. There is not one saved who is not in it. There is not one in it who is not saved. The guarantee of this is that the same one does both the saving and the adding to the church. The church is the saved." [1]

When we speak of the undenominational church, therefore, it is to this body of saved people that we point. Those who compose it are determined by the Lord, not man, including those unknown to us. "The Lord knows those who are his" (2 Timothy 2:19). It may also exclude some that we, in human judgment, would put within the borders of the Kingdom of God. It is not the sum total of all denominations, nor may its boundaries be limited by a personal concept that any of us has of the "brotherhood." There

20

is a brotherhood of the saints, but Christ, not man, is the judge of those within that fellowship. It is our purpose to explore the ramifications of this concept as we seek to redig the well of biblical truth.

Some vital questions must be asked as we approach our subject. Is undenominational Christianity a valid quest? If so, is it really desirable in this century to seek to achieve the goal implied in the principle? Is it even possible in a world of denominationalism to be just a Christian? How can we be undenominational when, through our constant association with others, the sectarianism of our religious neighbors intrudes itself upon our thinking and affects our actions? To these and related questions we will address ourselves in succeeding chapters.

Although the church is "built upon the foundation of the apostles and prophets, Christ Jesus himself being the cornerstone" (Ephesians 2:20), we ought not to assume that the early Christians completely escaped the scourge of sectarianism. A budding factionalism was evident when the Hellenistic Jewish Christians in Jerusalem murmured against the native Hebrews because they felt that their widows were neglected in the daily distribution of material help (Acts 6:1-6). Fortunately, the spirit of love and the wisdom of the apostles stamped out the threat.

Paul's testimony in his epistles and Luke's history in Acts attest to a denominational spirit threatening the very existence of the church in the circumcision controversy. Some Jewish Christians contended that before one could become a Christian he must first embrace Judaism. Again, wisdom, patience, and love seem to have been the antidote to the difficulty.

Sectarianism is seen most clearly within the congregation at Corinth. After having planted the church and labored with the disciples for a year and a half, Paul still found it necessary to write these brethren. "It has been reported to me by Chloe's people that there is quarreling among you, my brethren. What I mean is that each one of you says, 'I belong to Paul,' or 'I belong to Apollos,' or 'I belong to Cephas,' or 'I belong to Christ.' Is Christ divided? Was Paul crucified for you? Or were you baptized in the name of Paul?" (1 Corinthians 1:11-13). In this instance Christians were attaching themselves to different leaders and erecting barriers designed to denominate themselves and exclude others. Paul counsels each one to simply follow Jesus.

Perhaps, therefore, we should not be surprised to discover sectarianism in our day on a larger scale than is discernible in apostolic times. In form, however, it is much more clearly marked than is apparent in the early church. The term **denomination** is accepted without apology by most religious groups. Therefore, if we are to determine how to be Christians without being part of a denomination, we must first establish what it takes to make a denomination.

A denomination is a group of professed Christians with an existence that is not identical to the entire body of Christ. At best it is but part of the church, having separated itself by its actions from other disciples of Christ. At worst it may be totally outside the limits of the Christian faith, and hence, it may be argued, is not a denomination at all since it is not even Christian. However, **denomination** is here used in the popular sense to apply to all groups that call Jesus Lord.

Accepting this broad definition, what are the characteristics of a denomination? There are at least five, although not every denomination possesses all. To the extent that any of these marks are found, the body in question is a denomination.

A religious group is denominational if it has **a legislative or executive organization foreign to God's word**. Most denominations have human structures which regulate the teachings, policies, and practices of the bodies. They vary from the hierarchical government of Catholicism to those organizations in which most of the decision-making process resides in the congregation. That which makes a body denominational is the inter-congregational authority which reduces the autonomy (or self government) of the local unit. Any congregation which is unwilling to surrender its authority to the degree demanded by the denomination is automatically excluded from its fellowship.

A religious group is denominational if it has **an authoritative creed** which serves as a discipline for the body or is regarded as an official explanation of the Scriptures. The creed may be the sum total of pronouncements of the church head, the church councils, and historical confessions, or it may be embodied in a single writing called a confession, discipline, manual, or catechism. That which makes it a creed is not its interpretation of Scripture, but the official manner with which it speaks authoritatively of the doctrinal positions of the denomination. The book you are reading represents the personal viewpoint of the author. Were it to be officially accepted as the position of any group of people, it would become a creed. Some people are ignorant of the contents of the creed of their denomination and may feel, therefore, that they are not governed by it. But the congregations of which they are a part are directed by the creed, and the teaching set forth from the pulpits usually reflects the official point of view. To the extent that one is loyal to his denomination he is under the influence of the creed by which it is governed, even if he has never personally read it.

A religious body is denominational if it has **a basic doctrine which contradicts the word of God**. At this point virtually every religious body would claim innocence. Most people are where they are because they believe that their denomination is essentially correct in doctrine. Yet there obviously is a point at which a religious body ceases to be the church of God, even as John labeled those Gnostics of his day as the antichrist because they denied that Jesus is the Christ (1 John 2:22). The danger to be avoided in applying this test is that of taking an arbitrary set of guidelines which may be both too inclusive and too exclusive and declaring that all who do not conform to them are denominational because they subscribe to religious error. This problem will be dealt with later in our study.

A religious group is denominational if it wears **a distinctive name** which "denominates" it and separates it from others seeking to follow Christ. Ordinarily such a title is also without biblical authorization. It is obvious that many of the names used in the religious world are intended to mark those who wear them as a separate people, not just separate from the world, but separate from other disciples. This symptom of denominationalism is usually easy to recognize. However, it is also possible for a sect to adopt a biblical term and employ it in a denominational way. Could anyone deny that this is the case with that denomination which calls itself "The Church of the Living God, the Pillar and Ground of the Truth"? The phrase is biblical (1 Timothy 3:15), but the application is totally denominational. As used in the Bible it is simply a description of the family of God and is not intended as the official name of the church. It is, therefore, important that those seeking to be just Christians not only "speak as the oracles of God," but their words should also reflect a non-sectarian viewpoint.

Finally, a religious group is denominational if it possesses a **sectarian attitude**. This is the party spirit in which one's first allegiance is to his group rather than to Christ or the undenominational body for which he died. The Corinthian difficulties were rooted in a sectarian spirit. Some were following Paul or Apollos or Peter, giving them their first loyalty. But it is also possible

23

that those who declared they belonged to Christ were guilty of sectarianism. David Lipscomb comments on 1 Corinthians 1:12:

"Others still claimed to ignore all teachers and to be of Christ. This could be done in a partisan spirit. To ignore the teachers sent of Christ, and while doing this to claim to be of Christ, was to be a party." [2]

For one to assert that he is just a follower of Jesus is not conclusive evidence that he is not also sectarian. His claims must be measured against his actions. Self-examination respecting our attitudes is extremely important because those with the party spirit are usually the last to recognize it. Some of the worst sectarians are those who are most vocal in declaring that they and those with them alone constitute the church of the Lord. It should be observed that a sectarian attitude discernible among some within a fellowship may not characterize all in that group. A congregation of Christians may have a problem with the party spirit while a number, even a majority, are truly free in Christ.

As we approach this examination of undenominational Christianity, let us plumb the well to its depth, bypassing the accumulated teachings of generations, that we may truly be **Christians only** in word, in thought, in deed.

## FOOTNOTES

1. Cecil May, Jr., "Undenominational Christianity," **Firm Foundation,** June 10, 1969.

2. David Lipscomb, **A Commentary on the New Testament Epistles, Vol. II, First Corinthians** (Nashville: Gospel Advocate, 1956), p. 27.

# CHAPTER 2

# THE RESTORATION MOVEMENT

The Bogomils (Friends of God) of Bosnia, the Plymouth Brethren of England, the Evangelical Christians of Russia—what do these religious efforts stretched over the world and across the centuries have in common? Each was an effort in its own way to restore the Christianity of the first century. History is replete with stories of courageous men and women, who, often in the face of intense persecution, have sought a return to the pure religion of Jesus Christ. While the world is well acquainted with the various reformatory efforts of the sixteenth century resulting in the Protestant Reformation it is not so familiar with the accounts of those who sought to bypass the centuries of religious departures to go back to the Source. [1]

This investigation of undenominational Christianity is written against the background of a movement to reproduce the church of the apostolic period in our day. Originating in the early nineteenth century in what was then the western United States, it has usually been called the **Reformation of the Nineteenth Century** or the **Restoration Movement**. Its leaders did not attempt to establish another denomination, and, in fact, uncompromisingly condemned sectarianism in all forms. A brief history of the Restoration Movement is here given for those readers who may be unfamiliar with it. Those wishing a more exhaustive examination of the subject are directed to the standard historical works of the effort. [2]

Though all of us are familiar with the enigmatic expression of Leonardo da Vinci's "Mona Lisa," there are few who from memory could describe the background of the portrait. Yet the setting of the painting, though not its focal point, is vital to its beauty. Likewise, some knowledge of the history of the Restoration Movement is necessary if we are to appreciate the attempt of these people to be Christians **only**. Although this writing is not primarily a book of history, the historical development of the undenominational concept in the effort will be traced and numerous historical allusions will be made. It is not easy for disciples of Jesus in any period to be simply Christians as all of us are influenced by our surroundings and tend to allow our thinking to be shaped by contemporary attitudes. The Restoration Movement represents a determined struggle to reproduce the Christian religion of the first century in our day. A vital element of that faith is the restoration of non-sectarian Christianity.

How to designate those people in the movement we shall describe poses a problem. Since the movement is somewhat fragmented, it seems wise not to apply those biblical terms designating the whole body of Christ to a fellowship of congregations smaller than the sum total of the saved. To do so might be construed as implying that only those churches so specified constitute the entire family of God. In the early years the people of the Reformation of the Nineteenth Century were variously spoken of as "Disciples of Christ," "Christian Church," or "churches of Christ." The terms were used interchangeably. Today the phrases denote specific elements of the movement, and are frequently employed in a sectarian sense. Since this book is a study of the entire kingdom of God on earth, including those disciples in our land and others of whom none of us may be aware, our investigation will seek to avoid the sectarian use of biblical terminology.

Still, it is necessary to choose a descriptive term for those involved in the stream of this effort to return to the original religion of Christ. Our choice is the **Restoration Movement**. It may be argued that after nearly two centuries of history it is no longer a movement. Its critics would say it has stagnated. Yet anyone familiar with this effort knows immediately to whom the expression refers. In a sense it is a circumlocution designed to describe a people who do not constitute the whole body of Christ without applying to them a biblical phrase such as "church of Christ" whose meaning might be misconstrued by the reader. Moreover, this is also a study of varying attitudes toward undenominational Christianity within the entire movement, not a single segment of it. For these reasons, although it may seem an anachronism to some of our readers, the term **Restoration**

**Movement** has been chosen as the most precise descriptive designation of the effort as a whole.

The Restoration Movement was actually a coalescence of several efforts to return to apostolic Christianity. While two were of particular importance, the impact of the others should not be ignored. The first of these, sometimes termed the **Christian Connection**, was itself a fusion of three separate attempts to go back to the teachings of the early church. In 1793 James O'Kelly of Virginia led a revolt against the authoritarian domination of Francis Asbury in the Methodist Church. His followers, calling themselves **Republican Methodists**, adopted "Five Cardinal Principles" in which they accepted the Lord Jesus Christ as the only head of the church, the name Christian to the exclusion of all party and sectarian names, the Holy Bible, or the Scriptures of the Old and New Testaments as their only creed, and Christian character or vital piety as the sole test of fellowship. Rice Haggard was the one who suggested the name Christian and in 1801 the group adopted the name Christian Church.

In that same year there also began in New England a reformatory effort led by two Baptist preachers, Elias Smith and Dr. Abner Jones. A congregation was planted at Lyndon, Vermont, with the members calling themselves simply Christians. They rejected all sectarian names and accepted the New Testament as their only religious authority. As was true of the O'Kelly group, sincere piety was made the only test of fellowship. Smith began a religious paper called the **Herald of Gospel Liberty**. Unfortunately, he himself went into Unitarianism for a time and the effort itself became tainted with that philosophy.

In the meantime, the Second Great Awakening was sweeping the states west of the Appalachian Mountains. Thousands attended great emotional revivals which cut across the denominational lines. The greatest of these was in 1801 at Cane Ridge, Kentucky, at which an estimated 20,000 to 30,000 people were present. Serving the host congregation, the Cane Ridge Presbyterian Church, was Barton W. Stone. He and four other Presbyterian preachers soon became disenchanted with the narrowness of their Calvinistic doctrine. When one of them was officially charged by the Kentucky Synod with heresy, the five withdrew and in 1803 established the Springfield Presbytery. The fifteen churches organized in this new Presbyterian body became increasingly uncomfortable in their position, and, so, on June 28, 1804, issued a most remarkable document entitled "The Last

27

Will and Testament of the Springfield Presbytery." By its issuance the presbytery was officially dissolved and a call was made for other bodies to do likewise. The Bible was recognized as "the only sure guide to heaven." In that document is found the germ of undenominational Christianity, the theme of this book. The name **Christian** was adopted and the congregations were called Christian Churches, although their foes often dubbed them "New Lights." Unfortunately, two of Stone's co-workers were swept into the Shaker movement while two others soon returned to the Presbyterians. But the groundwork had been laid and under the direction of Stone the Christians soon made considerable progress in Kentucky and Ohio. They were strongly revivalistic and adopted the mourner's bench type of religion. At the same time they continued to draw closer to the apostolic pattern as they sought to return to biblical authority for their practices. They regarded the union of all believers in Christ as of prime importance.

In the next decade a loose relationship developed among the three efforts we have described. The **Herald of Gospel Liberty** reported the news of each and there was an interchange of correspondence and preaching, especially between the O'Kelly and New England movements. Many of the Virginia Christians moved across the mountains and associated themselves with the Stone effort. One of these was Rice Haggard, who first suggested to Stone the use of the name **Christian** as he had done earlier with the Republican Methodists. There were some doctrinal differences within the Christian Connection, one of them relating to baptism. The O'Kelly people did not practice immersion, the New Englanders did (although they did not insist on it), and the Kentucky Christians soon came to believe that the Scriptures taught immersion. By 1826 virtually all of the Stone element had been immersed.

When the Stone group merged with the effort led by the Campbells in 1832, a number in the Christian Connection refused to follow. The Unitarianism of those in New England and different attitudes toward baptism were impediments. Most of the New England people and many of the O'Kelly group remained outside the Restoration Movement. Additionally, some of the churches associated with Stone refused to follow his lead. The remaining congregations continued to be identified as the Christian Church or Christian Connection. In 1931 this body merged with the Congregational Church to become the Congregational Christian Church. This denomination, in turn, consolidated in 1957 with the Evangelical and Reformed Church (itself the result

28

of a merger) to form the United Church of Christ. This body should not be confused with any of those "churches of Christ" with their historical roots in the Restoration Movement.

The second major branch of the Restoration Movement began a few years after Stone had launched his effort. Thomas Campbell, a Presbyterian clergyman from North Ireland, immigrated to the United States in 1807 and was given an assignment by his denomination in western Pennsylvania. However, he was soon suspended from the ministry for asserting that there is only human authority for creeds and confessions of faith, and for offering the Lord's supper to other Presbyterians than those in his own sect. After deciding to disassociate himself from the Presbyterians, he assembled a sympathetic group of people and organized "The Christian Association of Washington" (Pennsylvania) in 1809. At its direction he wrote its **Declaration and Address** in which he enunciated the principles upon which the Restoration Movement was later to proceed. Briefly stated, the document affirmed the sole authority of the Holy Scriptures, the individual Christian's responsibility before God and the right of private judgment, and the evil of sectarianism. It pointed the way to peace and unity in the body of Christ through conformity to the Holy Scriptures. These were essentially the same concepts being preached by the Christian Connection. The major difference between the two groups as they developed was that those with Campbell placed greater emphasis on biblical authority and less on union while the converse was true of Stone and his associates. It was Thomas Campbell who, in forming the Christian Association, proposed the motto that has frequently been repeated in the Restoration Movement, "Where the Scriptures speak, we speak; and where the Scriptures are silent, we are silent."

Campbell's son, Alexander, came from Scotland, where he had been attending college, to join his father about the same time the **Declaration and Address** was issued. He had gone through a period of soul searching as had his father, and had independently reached a similar point of view. He was destined in the next few years to assume the mantle of leadership and to become, by any estimate, the most dominant figure in the entire history of the Restoration Movement. Earnest study of the Scriptures convinced him that biblical baptism is by immersion. The Christian Association was soon constituted into the Brush Run Church with virtually the entire group being immersed. For several years, the Campbells cast their lot with the Redstone Baptist Association, but when doctrinal tensions mounted, they withdrew and associated themselves with the Mahoning Baptist Association in the Western Reserve of Ohio. The name of Alexander Campbell was soon known throughout the West. In 1820 he and Presbyterian John Walker engaged in a public debate on baptism, the first of a number of discussions destined to thrust Campbell before the public eye and give him considerable influence, especially among the Baptists. In 1823 he launched his first publication, the **Christian Baptist,** in which he laid down in brilliant logic the principles of the Restoration Movement. Calling for a return to "the ancient order of things," he examined in minute detail the nature of the apostolic church. His bitter attack on the establishment, especially the clergy, created many personal enemies. Between 1820 and 1830 it became increasingly evident that Campbell's teachings were dividing the Baptists of the West into two groups—the Orthodox Calvinists and the Reforming Baptists led by Campbell. Campbell's writings went everywhere and affected thousands among all religious groups, including those of the Christian Connection.

In 1827 Walter Scott was chosen by the Mahoning Association as its evangelist. Influenced by Campbell, he proclaimed with astounding success throughout the Western Reserve the doctrine of immersion for the remission of sins. Meanwhile, Campbell's views spread widely into adjoining states. In 1830 the Mahoning Association dissolved itself as a Baptist organization because of the conviction of its members that it had no biblical basis for existence. The North District Baptist Association in Kentucky did likewise the next year. Those aligning themselves with the doctrinal position of the Campbells came to be called Reformers or Disciples, or, by their enemies, "Campbellites."

The spread of the Stone and Campbell movements brought them into the same geographic areas and compelled the leaders to examine their positions in the light of their plea. Both pled for unity on the basis of the Scriptures alone. A series of unity meetings which began in 1831 soon resulted in an amalgamation of forces throughout the West. As neither group had any denominational machinery, no formal steps were taken to effect union, but as they stood on the same platform and had sufficient love for one another, true unity was accomplished, with the exception of those churches of the Christian Connection that refused to go along with the merger. No single descriptive term was applied to those in this consolidated effort. They were usually called disciples or Christians while the local congregation would be described as a "church of Christ" or "Christian Church."

There were other tributaries in the Restoration Movement. Most of them have been so overshadowed by the Stone and Campbell efforts that few are aware of the role they played in the return to the Bible in the early nineteenth century.

In 1819, John Wright, an Indiana Baptist, offered a resolution to the Blue River Association to dispense with all party names in favor of biblical expressions such as Christians. He called for acceptance of God's word as the sole authority of faith and practice, and by 1821 there were no longer Baptist Churches in his region. On the same basis he effected a union with fifteen Tunker congregations which was followed in turn by a union with the Christians associated with Stone.

A similar movement was begun in 1809 in the vicinity of Tompkinsville, Kentucky, by John Mulkey on the basis of "the Bible alone." These churches also later became a part of the Stone group.

In Georgia, Christian Herman Dasher, a Lutheran immigrant, found his way out of religious error about 1819. The congregations in the vicinity of Valdosta are the result of this work begun separately from the Stone and Campbell efforts.

The restoration effort in Great Britain was independent of that in the United States, although Campbell's influence came to be felt in England and Scotland as an interrelationship between the parallel movements developed.

Since the Springfield Presbytery issued its "Last Will and Testament," there have been many distinct attempts to return to to the Bible as our only source of religious authority. They continue to be discovered throughout the world, vividly illustrating that the restoration plea is not uniquely American, but is as universal as the gospel message itself. Those who on their own find their way out of the labyrinth of religious error are as truly a part of the undenominational body of Christ as any of those disciples who are indebted to the Campbells and Stones of another generation.

The decade of the 1830's found the people of the Restoration increasingly separated from their religious neighbors. Until then they were a group of efforts calling for all men to unite on the basis of the Bible alone. As these efforts coalesced, they became a real force and friendship or indifference on the part of others turned into antagonism. After all, their plea if truly carried out would result in the destruction of denominationalism. The 1830's were also a period of reexamination of the teachings of the Word. With the diverse backgrounds of these people it is small wonder that they did not always see eye to eye on matters of interpretation. The nineteenth century reformers did not reach their conclusions overnight. They had laboriously dug their way through the maze of theology of their day in quest of the pure water given by Jesus. By the 1830's they had not found all of the answers, nor have we, for that matter, found them all today. Restoration is a never-ending struggle to capture the essence of the religion of Christ.

Between the 1832 consolidation of the Stone and Campbell forces and the year 1850, the number of Christians associated with the Restoration Movement grew from an estimated 20,000 to 200,000, most of them in the states of Kentucky, Indiana, Ohio, Missouri, and Illinois. They published at least twenty-eight religious papers and founded three Christian colleges. This growth did not result from the clanking of denominational machinery or an organized missionary society, but from an unblushing zeal to tell others the story of Jesus.

Nevertheless, the harmony of these Christians was soon threatened by an ominous cloud. In his earlier writings Alexander Campbell had strongly opposed any organized society to carry out the work of the church. In 1849, however, he consented to become the first president of the newly founded American Christian Missionary Society. Numerous brethren felt he had abandoned his previously stated principles and there was strong opposition to the society as being without biblical authorization. The controversy engendered nearly caused the society to go under in the 1870's and threatened the unity of the Restoration Movement for the first time. There was a growing fear of ecclesiasticism and a concern that the society might destroy the autonomy of the local church. This was denied by its proponents, and yet the denominational structure of present day Disciples of Christ is the ultimate outgrowth of the society established in 1849. The controversy also brought into focus varying attitudes toward biblical interpretation and pointed to the need, still present, of the proper approach to interpretation of the Scriptures.

The Civil War was a traumatic period in the Restoration Movement, as it was for other religious groups. Some Christians were pro-Union, others pro-Confederate, while a sizeable number, including influential leaders, totally opposed the participation of Christians in war. The war between the states did not divide the Restoration Movement, but it seriously strained relations and was a factor in later division.

The post-war period saw an increasing desire for religious recognition among Restoration elements. The denominational idea was emerging among some of these undenominational Christians, and it is at this time that some in the movement began a more critical examination of the undenominational concept. Few acknowledged being denominational, but symptoms of the disease were appearing at an alarming rate.

In this same period a second major controversy began to rock the Restoration Movement. Until 1859 none of the congregations had used an instrument of music in public worship. Most prominent leaders, including Campbell, opposed its use on a biblical ground. But in the 1870's and 1880's an increasing number of churches introduced the instrument with resulting division in hundreds of churches. In some cases the proponents departed to establish a congregation using the instrument, while in other instances the opponents left because they could not worship in good conscience where the instrument was played. Those who opposed the instrument often opposed the society, while the proponents of one were frequently supporters of the other. There was, however, a sizeable number who supported the society but who steadfastly opposed the instrument. By 1900 defenders of the middle-of-the-road position had disappeared. The music problem led to division more often than did the society difficulty because it involved the conscience of the worshipper while the society did not. One did not have to agree with the society to associate with its adherents, but, for those conscientiously opposed to its use, the instrument precluded association in the closest fellowship of all, that of worship.

By 1890 there were two discernible camps in the Restoration Movement. The "progressives," whose position was championed by the **Christian Standard** and **Christian Evangelist** magazines, were more numerous in the North, while the "conservatives," influenced in great measure by the **Gospel Advocate**, were mostly in the South. Still, without a denominational organization there could be no formal divison and not all were yet fully aware of the critical situation. "Christian Church" and "Church of Christ" were still applied interchangeably to congregations, regardless of their views in the controversies. Increasingly, however, the "conservatives" adopted the exclusive use of "Church of Christ" while the "progressive" element tended to favor "Disciples" or "Christian Church," although some of these congregations continued to call themselves "Church of Christ." In 1906 the United States government in its religious census report officially recognized the breach by listing them separately as "Disciples of Christ" and "Churches of Christ." By this date evidence of active fellowship between them was difficult to find.

The first decade of the twentieth century saw the emergence of a small but significant number of leaders among the "progressives" espousing the views of theological liberalism. Led by the Disciples Divinity House, the Campbell Institute, and the **Christian Century** magazine, they attacked the inerrency of the written word of God and called in question its absolute authority. Acceptance of the unimmersed into fellowship began to be practiced and a new tension became apparent. The **Christian Standard** maintained a conservative position on these issues while the **Christian Evangelist** was increasingly friendly to the views of the theological liberals. The United Christian Missionary Society and its associated International Convention became the centers of controversy. This organizational machinery came increasingly under the control of the more liberal element with the result that in 1927 the North American Christian Convention was set up to express another point of view. In an attempt to promote understanding the International Convention authorized a Commission on Restudy of the Disciples of Christ. Its 1946 report reflected the deep cleavage among the "progressives." A second major division within the Restoration Movement over theological liberalism, open membership (acceptance of the unimmersed), and related matters was now evident. A. T. DeGroot declared that in 1955 the rupture had become complete with the establishment of what he sarcastically called, "Church of Christ Number Two." [3]

In 1968 the liberal Disciples officially restructured themselves into the Christian Church (Disciples of Christ) with a frankly denominational name and organization, thus abandoning all claim to an undenominational status. Those "progressive" churches that have refused to align themselves with the Disciples are known congregationally as "Christian Churches" or "Churches of Christ," and sometimes are called "independents" for purposes of identification.

In the meantime the "conservative" congregations that refused to use the instrument in worship faced a rebuilding period following the first major division. Numerical growth was rapid, especially after World War II when greater strength made possible the sending of workers into many parts of the world. Controversies over such matters as communion cups, Bible classes, and congregational cooperation sometimes marred these efforts, resulting in several small factions. One writer claims to find over twenty such groups among the "conservatives." [4] While it may be that this number can be found, most are small elements, and it is probable that fully eighty percent of the "conservatives" are in the mainstream. Furthermore, it should be recognized that among autonomous congregations there is virtually no defense against the one who separates himself and starts a faction over a minor issue. Numerically the division may be insignificant, yet it might still be counted as one of the "twenty." Although no complete statistics are available, it is generally recognized that the "conservatives" currently outnumber both the Disciples and the "independents." [5]

The restoration story is a thrilling one etched with sadness because of the internal difficulties of the last hundred years. These problems do not invalidate the plea to return to the New Testament, but do demonstrate the need to plumb the depths of the Scriptures more fully to determine the message of Christ and his apostles. Divisions have not resulted from God's word, but from man's misapplication of it. An element sorely neglected in the Restoration Movement has been an exhaustive examination of the meaning of undenominational Christianity. One wonders if the divisiveness that has sometimes been apparent would not have been greatly diminished had this principle been completely understood. It is to this end that your attention is directed in this book.

## FOOTNOTES

1. One of the best examinations of restoration efforts is **The Pilgrim Church** (London: Pickering and Inglis, 1931) by E. H. Broadbent. Although not an in-depth study and deficient in some areas, it gathers under a single cover the stories of many attempts through the centuries to return to the primitive pattern.

2. The three most comprehensive historical examinations of the Restoration Movement are **The Search for the Ancient Order** (Nashville: Gospel Advocate, 1949, 1950 - 2 vols.) by Earl Irvin West, **Christians Only** (Cincinnati: Standard Publishing, 1962) by James DeForest Murch, and **The Disciples of Christ: A History** (St. Louis: Bethany Press 1948, revised 1958) by W. E. Garrison and A. T. DeGroot. The first is written from the perspective of

the "conservatives" and carries the history to 1906. It is especially complete in detailing the first major division. The second is written from the standpoint of the "independents," but probably gives the broadest coverage of the movement as a whole. The third reflects the attitude of the Disciples, and like the second brings the history well into the twentieth century.

3. Alfred T. DeGroot, **Church of Christ Number Two** (Birmingham, England: Birmingham Printers, 1956), p. 4.

4. W. Carl Ketcherside, "Church of Christ Party," **Mission Messenger,** December, 1959, p. 2.

5. James DeForest Murch, **Christians Only** (Cincinnati: Standard Publishing, 1962), p. 309.

# CHAPTER 3
# DOCTRINAL PRESUPPOSITIONS

A straight line is the shortest distance between two points. Every student of the most elemental form of Euclidian geometry is aware of this truth. Without this proposition the study of plane geometry would be impossible. Yet, as every student also knows, this simple statement is an axiom, an unprovable assumption. It is a presupposition, essential to all conclusions which follow.

Every system of thought is based on presuppositions. To illustrate, before two people can intelligently discuss whether the Bible is the word of God, they must agree that there is a supreme being. Similarly, the teaching of original sin was the doctrinal presupposition on which the practice of infant baptism was initially introduced. If two people cannot agree that babies are born contaminated with the guilt of original sin, they are unlikely to concur on the necessity of infant baptism. If the dogma of original sin is correct, the essentiality of the baptism of babies follows. Those groups which continue to observe infant baptism after altering their views to discount original sin are much like the man who builds a house upon a foundation and then expects it to stand after its base collapses.

Inherent in the concept of undenominational Christianity are certain doctrinal presuppositions. To those unwilling to grant their validity the very investigation of this subject will appear futile. We must, therefore, inquire whether the tenets upon which the undenominational idea rests are basically sound. Is another form of Christianity desirable? For that matter, is undenominational Christianity even possible in the twentieth century?

Since the subject is being considered from the historical perspective of the Restoration Movement, an examination of the objectives of that effort as set forth by its earliest leaders should be made. Von Kirk lists three principles envisioned by Alexander Campbell as fundamental to the movement. They are (1) the conversion of the world, (2) the union of all Christians, and (3) the restoration of primitive Christianity. He then adds, "The history of the Disciples of Christ may be written in the terms of these principles." [1] Historically, the second and third of these objectives were usually stressed, although the conversion of the world was always a fundamental goal, even if unstated.

From the beginning both Barton W. Stone and the Campbells stressed the importance of Christian union. It was their mutual emphasis on this objective which was a dominant factor in the fusion of their forces in the 1830's. We must inquire, therefore, if the concept of Christian union is one of the presuppositions of undenominational Christianity. It should be observed that were Christian union to be effected upon a basis pleasing to Christ we would in essence have undenominational Christianity. Viewed from one perspective undenominational Christianity is the absence of sectarianism. If there were but one body of Christians the whole question raised in this book would be academic.

However, doctrinal considerations enter here. Was the Catholic Church of the middle ages undenominational simply because most professing Christians were of that faith? If it was an apostate church, as many affirm, then the unity factor alone is insufficient to mark it as the body of Christ. Unity and undenominational Christianity are not necessarily the same. Ideally they should be, but in fact you may have one without the other.

Practically speaking, the restoration call for all followers of Jesus to unite did not materialize. Nor, realistically, are we to suppose that all of Christendom will now become one. We must, therefore, inquire whether for those disciples who strive to be **just Christians** the plea of Christian union is a doctrinal presupposition to their undenominational status. We must respond in the negative. Were that true we would have to conclude that when the first Christian "sects" appeared at the end of the apostolic age, the rest of the church, still holding firm to the apostolic moorings, became sectarian because others had severed the unity of the church. While Christian union is assuredly

38

desirable, it is possible for one to be undenominational without enjoying the spiritual fellowship of others who seek to follow Christ.

The other objective, which was viewed as the means of attaining Christian union, the restoration of New Testament Christianity, is another matter. The principle of undenominational Christianity presumes that Christ's followers should be united and that the type of unity described in the New Testament is the ideal. Of course, the unity of the apostolic church was not perfect as we observe in the circumcision conflict (Acts 15). But the sectarian system we know today did not then exist. In spite of tensions between Jew and Gentile, there was still but one body. All were Christians **only.** If we are to return to this ideal condition we must restore Christianity as it was known in the first century, at least so far as its fundamental elements are concerned. Undenominational Christianity is meaningless apart from the restoration ideal. If one is unwilling to grant that the church in its essential nature should be restored to what it was in the first century, why should he acknowledge that there is any virtue in a non-sectarian system? Some would favor a Catholic Church with all Christians united in that universal body. Others would prefer a church in which each person is free to believe as he wishes regardless of Bible teaching. Still others would vote to retain the present denominational system because in it each one can find his niche according to his outlook and temperament. Only when one sees the desirability of a return to early Christianity does the undenominational plea become meaningful.

But, is the restoration plea valid? Viewed from a biblical perspective we discover from time to time in the Old Testament a call for a return to an ideal, a way of life which had been forsaken. This was the message of both the oral and written prophets. During his reign King Hezekiah of Judah set in motion a great movement to restore the Jewish religion which had degenerated during the time of Ahaz, his father (2 Kings 18:1-6). In the following century, after the nation had once more lapsed into idolatry, Hezekiah's great-grandson, Josiah, instituted another restoration under the leadership of Hilkiah the priest (2 Kings 22:3-23:25). It should be observed that had the people not departed from God a restoration effort would not have been necessary. The very idea of restoration presupposes a prior departure from truth.

In the New Testament Jesus suggests the restoration principle in His discussion of divorce. When His disciples inquired about the Jewish practice of putting away wives "for any cause," Jesus calls them back to the pre-Mosaic ethic as authority for His teaching (Matthew 19:3-9). In His denunciation of the practices of the scribes and Pharisees He shows the need for a restoration of the spirit of the law of Moses without in any way denying the essentiality of the letter of the law in which the spirit was expressed (Matthew 23).

Fundamental to the question, "Is the plea to restore New Testament Christianity in the twentieth century valid?" is still another inquiry, "Is Christianity of divine origin?" If it is human in its inception there is no particular value in restoring its human values. But if its principles are a matter of divine revelation we are dealing with perfect concepts which never need updating. Since God is omniscient those maxims which He reveals can never be improved upon. True, the application of divine truths will vary from time to time and culture to culture, but the verities themselves remain unchanged. Therefore, when man departs from them it is essential that they be restored. Thus, Christianity by its very nature as a religion of divine origin validates the restoration principle.

The golden rule is a case in point. Cannot all Christians agree that the golden rule is (1) not being widely followed, and (2) its use needs to be restored? Granted that in this case we are in the realm of ethics, this at least establishes the necessity of restoring some elements of the religion of Jesus. The real question relates not to the validity of the restoration principle, but to which elements in primitive Christianity need to be restored.

Dr. Alfred T. DeGroot in his book, **The Restoration Principle,** has analyzed from an historical perspective efforts at restoration through the centuries. He concludes that a restoration of Christianity is needed and he lists these objectives: (1) the ends, aims or purposes rather than the means to those ends; (2) an enlargement of existing unity in the Christian family; (3) the recapturing of the optimism and expectancy of the early church; (4) the grand concept of freedom; (5) what the qualified judgment of sincere Christians can agree is essential to worship and life; and (6) a conquering spiritual life.[2] Upon much of this most of us can agree, but DeGroot stops short of conceding that there is also found in the New Testament a pattern of the apostolic church which should be restored. In fact, he specifically denies that such a pattern exists and as partial proof of his position argues that in the post-apostolic period the idea of the restoration of the church is not to be found in the writings of the church fathers. [3]

We have already observed that the restoration concept is found only when there has been a departure from the faith. If we do not find the restoration of the church mentioned in the second century by such men as Ignatius, Polycarp, and Justin Martyr, it is that these men did not feel the need for restoration. They doubtless did not believe that what had been revealed had been lost, except for the departures of heretics. A gradual drift from the primitive pattern is seldom detected until it is far advanced and it is only then that restoration is called for. Therefore, the testimony of the post-apostolic fathers has little bearing one way or the other on the restoration ideal.

But is there a discernible pattern of the church evident in the New Testament? Paul, in his first letter to Timothy, affirms that there is. In chapter one he discusses doctrinal matters, in chapter two worship, and in chapter three church organization. He then admonishes Timothy, "I hope to come to you soon, but I am writing these instructions to you so that, if I am delayed, you may know **how one ought to behave in the household of God,** which is the church of the living God, the pillar and bulwark of the truth" (1 Timothy 3:14,15). In effect he declares that his divinely revealed writings constitute a pattern for the household of God.

However, many critics of restorationism point to the disagreements among those who claim to follow a pattern as proof that none exists. The misapplication of biblical principles resulting in erroneous conclusions, though, is not sufficient proof that the principles themselves are invalid. It is true that among those who through the centuries have sought restoration there has been considerable disparity of views. Part of this results from seeking restoration in one area while neglecting another. If one group seeks a restoration of the plan of the church and another a restoration of commitment to Christ, the two will disagree because the restoration of neither is complete.

Another factor, and one that has weighed heavily in disagreements in the Restoration Movement, is that some tend to claim patterns of action that do not exist. The mere presence of lights in an upper room during a period of worship (Acts 20:8) is no evidence that we cannot worship without lights. Restoration Movement teachers have long correctly insisted on biblical authority for religious action. They have taught that authority is determined by direct command, approved example, and necessary inference. But considerably more care needs to be given in interpreting the Bible and establishing what God actually requires. Taken at face value the lights in the upper room constitute an approved example. If we mean by stating that authority is determined by example and that we are obligated to do whatever we have an example for, it follows that we must always worship with lights and in an upper room at that! Few so contend, but some have found such patterns in the New Testament with about as little justification as the lights at Troas.

The establishment of the New Testament pattern requires careful biblical interpretation. Separation must be made of that which is simply a cultural expression and what is a divinely revealed directive. It is certain that the Jews in the time of Jesus, or at least some of them, practiced ceremonial baptism. When Jesus baptized His disciples this was nothing strange to the people, yet we would mistakenly conclude that baptism is only a cultural expression since it was specifically commanded by Jesus and the New Testament writers. On the other hand, the holy kiss would seem to be a cultural practice which is not bound on us today. Admittedly the separation of incidentals from essentials is sometimes hard, but the difficulty itself does not argue that for this reason there is no pattern.

Just as the restoration concept is a presupposition of un-denominational Christianity, so there are also presuppositions underlying the restoration ideal. Failure to acknowledge the validity of these presuppositions is a major reason for some having rejected restorationism. Let us consider three of these. First, Christians are bound by the authority of Jesus in their faith and practice. This is established by the Great Commission in which Jesus states, "All authority in heaven and on earth has been given to me" (Matthew 28:18). Certainly the apostles and early Christians regarded themselves bound by that authority. Certainly most disciples of Jesus since that day have considered themselves bound by His teachings, not only as recounted in the gospels, but as revealed in written form by His apostles. Until the last hundred years few have questioned this presupposition.

A second presupposition is that the New Testament, as we know it, is the sole expression of that authority. Here we encounter more disagreement. Obviously in the early days of the church the authority of the apostles (who in turn taught by the authority of Christ) was expressed both orally and in writing. In the earliest days oral teaching certainly predominated since the New Testament books had not yet been written. We must acknowledge that were Peter or Paul to appear on the scene today we would be bound to accept their inspired oral utterances as quite as authoritative as their writings. Are there other ways in which God today communicates with us by revealing new truths or enlarging upon old ones? The Catholic position is that authority is vested in the church, which is the guardian, not only of the written word, but also of tradition, and that through her councils and pontiffs she is a revealer of truth. Others are convinced that we have latter-day prophets, or that in some subjective way the Lord communicates truths to the individual Christian. This certainly is the case with those who believe that Christians today have charismatic gifts. Still others inquire whether we can really know if the twenty-seven books of the New Testament are the only existing writings inspired by the Holy Spirit, and whether we can know that all of these were actually inspired. One writer inquires what our reaction would be if a twenty-eighth book, Paul's first letter to the church at Corinth (1 Corinthians 5:9), were to be discovered.

Personally, these questions, as well as similar ones not here mentioned, do not pose a major difficulty. It is not within the purview of this book to give an exhaustive critique of the restoration principle. These problems are cited to suggest that simplistic answers to a profound question should be not given.

The third presupposition, that the New Testament reveals a pattern of the church to be restored, has already been discussed. In recent years several writers associated with the Restoration Movement have called the restoration plea invalid on the ground that there is no pattern to be followed. W. E. Garrison in **Religion Follows the Frontier** rejects the restoration concept because of two presuppositions which he denies—that the apostolic church did not have a mixture of human influences and that the New Testament Scriptures present an inerrant picture of the early church. [4]

In effect Garrison is saying that there is no divine pattern in the New Testament because too much of the book is of human rather than divine origin. In the **Panel of Scholars Reports** of the Disciples of Christ, Ralph Wilburn spells this out in detail. He lists "five fundamental errors in the Disciple restoration plea." The first one is the false presupposition of the orthodox view of the Bible which considers it to be an infallible book. In his article he raises questions of higher criticism relating to the quest for the real historical Jesus. [5]

All of this boils down to a rejection of the restoration principle on the ground that the New Testament is not of divine origin. This means its writings contain divine truths, but they assuredly do not reveal a pattern from God since the twenty-seven books are largely of human inception.

Essentially, therefore, the fundamental objection to our third presupposition of restorationism—that the New Testament reveals a pattern of the church to be restored—is that the New Testament is not divinely inspired. But for one who believes that it has in fact come from God, the idea of a divinely revealed pattern is not only possible, but essential. Inspiration inevitably results in a pattern.

It is the position taken in this book that the New Testament is God's inspired revelation and that it accurately records the authoritative teachings of Jesus. On this basis we conclude that the restoration principle is fundamentally sound and that we must seek to restore every essential element of primitive Christianity, including those teachings relating to the church. This cannot be done without also restoring undenominational Christianity.

In our effort to restore the religion of the first century, let us be sure that we do not merely seek to restore the Restoration Movement. The Stones and Campbells of another day pointed others to Christ rather than to themselves. In a unity effort of a few years ago a young man stated that we need to roll back the clock to the time when there was unity. "We need to get back to the restoration leaders," he declared. In answer it was pointed out that we must return to Christ, not the Campbells. The great reformers of the past century can point us in the right direction as we seek to restore New Testament Christianity, but only God's word can give us the ultimate answers.

## FOOTNOTES

1. Hiram Von Kirk, **The Rise of the Current Reformation** (St. Louis: Christian Publishing Co., 1907), p. 118.

2. Alfred T. DeGroot, **The Restoration Principle** (St. Louis: Bethany Press, 1960), pp. 165-185.

3. **Ibid.**, p. 87.

4. Wilfred Ernest Garrison, **Religion Follows the Frontier** (New York and London: Harper and Brothers, 1931), pp. 40, 41.

44

5. Ralph G. Wilburn, "A Critique of the Restoration Principle," **The Panel of Scholars Reports, The Reformation Tradition,** (St. Louis: Bethany Press, 1971), Vol. 1, pp. 215-251.

# CHAPTER 4
# "WE WILL THAT THIS BODY DIE"

If in our quest for undenominational Christianity we would know where we are going, it is imperative that we learn where we have been. A study of the past illuminates the future. Through the centuries there have been numerous attempts to reproduce apostolic Christianity in its primitive simplicity. A study of the areas in which these efforts have succeeded or failed can benefit us in a similar endeavor.

The Reformation of the Nineteenth Century, or the Restoration Movement as it is better known, is the most significant of these efforts in modern times. Today thousands of congregations in the United States, Canada, and other nations owe their existence to men who a century and a half ago proclaimed the necessity of a return to New Testament Christianity. These churches bear the imprint of the thinking of these men. All of us are inevitably influenced by our teachers. Therefore, a study of the concept of undenominational Christianity as it developed in the Restoration Movement is essential if we are to appreciate the attitudes of these people as they sought to restore that aspect of the gospel message.

Two documents from the first decade of the nineteenth century must be examined first because of their importance in the development of thought in the Restoration Movement. Each contains the germ of the undenominational idea. The first is **The Last Will and Testament of the Springfield Presbytery.** It was issued June 28, 1804, at Cane Ridge, Kentucky, by the six men responsible for the existence of the presbytery.

Barton W. Stone, who was the most influential one in the group, tells what occurred:

"Under the name of Springfield Presbytery we went forward preaching, and constituting churches; but we had not worn our name more than one year, before we saw it savored of a party spirit. With the man-made creeds we threw it overboard, and took the name **Christian**—the name given to the disciples by divine appointment first at Antioch. We published a pamphlet on this name, written by Elder Rice Haggard, who had lately united with us. Having divested ourselves of all party creeds, and party names, and trusting alone in God, and the word of his grace, we became a by-word and laughing stock to the sects around; all prophesying our speedy annihilation. Yet from this period I date the commencement of that reformation, which has progressed to this day." [1]

In less than a year after the new presbytery had been formed, the last will and testament of the organization was issued. Several items in it indicate the attitude of the group relative to sectarianism and are noteworthy:

"The Presbytery of Springfield, sitting at Cane-ridge, in the county of Bourbon, being, through a gracious Providence, in more than ordinary bodily health, growing in strength and size daily; and in perfect soundness and composure of mind; but knowing that it is appointed for all delegated bodies once to die; and considering that the life of every such body is very uncertain, do make, and ordain this our last Will and Testament, in manner and form following, viz:

"**Imprimis.** We **will**, that this body die, be dissolved, and sink into union with the Body of Christ at large; for there is but one Body, and one Spirit, even as we are called in one hope of our calling.

"**Item.** We **will**, that our name of distinction, with its **Reverend** title, be forgotten, that there be but one Lord over God's heritage, and his name One.

"**Item.** We **will**, that our power of making laws for the government of the church, and executing them by delegated authority, forever cease; that the people may have free course to the Bible, and adopt **the law of the Spirit of life in Christ Jesus** . . . .

"**Item.** We **will,** that the people henceforth take the Bible as the only sure guide to heaven; and as many as are offended with other books, which stand in competition with it, may cast them into the fire if they choose; for it is better to enter into life having one book, than having many to be cast into hell . . . .

"**Item.** Finally we **will,** that all our **sister bodies** read their Bibles carefully, that they may see their fate there determined, and prepare for death before it is too late." [2]

This document is a clear rejection of sectarianism. The very right of denominational bodies to exist is denied. Moreover, the unity of the one divine church is asserted, and a call to union in that body issued. Truly, if all followers of Jesus would unite upon this platform we would in fact have undenominational Christianity. This did not occur, however, and eventually the Christians associated with Stone were forced to consider the difficult question of how one can be just a Christian when denominationalism is the order of the day.

How profound an impact the **Last Will and Testament** made is unknown, but certainly the principles expressed in it became the embodiment of the teaching of those who, having cast off the shackles of sectarianism, now went forth to proclaim the simple message of Jesus. Evangelistically inclined, they persuaded many to accept their plea, especially in Kentucky and adjoining states. By the time of the fusion with the forces led by the Campbells there were possibly ten thousand associated in this effort.

The second document of major importance in the restoration effort, and one of considerably more influence than the other, is the **Declaration and Address** of **The Christian Association of Washington,** authored by Thomas Campbell. The association was born August 17, 1809, and a group of twenty-one was appointed to work with Campbell in drawing up a statement of principles. The **Declaration and Address,** adopted September 7, 1809, was the result. It is a lengthy document deserving more careful analysis than can be given here. In it are stated the basic principles of the Restoration Movement. Beyond doubt it was the greatest work of Thomas Campbell's life. Several statements in it relate to our topic. After decrying the division of the age and calling for Christian unity, the **Declaration** lists thirteen propositions in which its principles are set forth.

"Prop. 1. That the Church of Christ upon earth is essentially, intentionally, and constitutionally one; consisting of all those in every place that profess their faith in Christ and obedience to him in all things according to the Scriptures, and that manifest the same by their tempers and conduct, and of none else; as none else can be truly and properly called Christians.

"2. That although the Church of Christ upon earth must necessarily exist in particular and distinct societies, locally separate one from another, yet there ought to be no schisms, no uncharitable divisions among them. They ought to receive each other as Christ Jesus hath also received them, to the glory of God. And for this purpose they ought all to walk by the same rule, to mind and speak the same thing; and to be perfectly joined together in the same mind, and in the same judgment.

"3. That in order to do this, nothing ought to be inculcated upon Christians as articles of faith; nor required of them as terms of communion, but what is expressly taught and enjoined upon them in the word of God. Nor ought anything to be admitted, as of Divine obligation, in their Church constitution and managements, but what is expressly enjoined by the authority of our Lord Jesus Christ and his apostles upon the New Testament Church; either in express terms or by approved precedent . . . .

"10. That division among the Christians is a horrid evil, fraught with many evils. It is antichristian, as it destroys the visible unity of the body of Christ; as if he were divided against himself, excluding and excommunicating a part of himself. It is antiscriptural, as being strictly prohibited by his sovereign authority; a direct violation of his express command. It is antinatural, as it excites Christians to contemn, to hate, and oppose one another, who are bound by the highest and most endearing obligations to love each other as brethren, even as Christ has loved them. In a word, it is productive of confusion and of every evil work . . . . " [3]

Note that in this paper the unity of the body of Christ is clearly stated—"the Church of Christ upon earth is essentially, intentionally, and constitutionally one; consisting of all those in every place that profess their faith in Christ and obedience to him in all things according to the Scriptures." This certainly is an undenominational definition of the church of God—it is a unity composed of all Christians. We should remember, however, that at this time Campbell was still a pedobaptist. His conception of those within the borders of the Kingdom embraced not only Presbyterians, but also Methodists, Lutherans, and perhaps even Catholics. Christian character was the basis of the right to wear the name Christian. It is likely that a few years later, after having adopted immersion as the biblical expression of baptism, he might have defined "Christian" in narrower terms. Be that as it may, the later view of the reformers on baptism materially affected their attitude as to the composition of the church of God.

The importance of Christian unity, with the authority of the scriptures as its standard, is distinctly set forth in this manifesto. It is coupled with a denuciation of sectarianism among Christians. Thus, the **Declaration and Address** set forth in a somewhat different way the same concept of Christianity and the same means of attaining Christian unity that had been earlier stressed in the **Last Will and Testament.** Yet Stone and Campbell reached their conclusions independently. With the arrival in New York from Scotland of Campbell's son, Alexander, on September 29, 1809, the leadership of the movement launched by the father in Washington soon passed into the hands of the younger man. Before this happened, however, the basic principles shaping the thinking of succeeding generations had been set forth in the **Declaration and Address.**

The second and third decades of the nineteenth century saw the development of two movements drawing large numbers from diverse religious backgrounds. The Stone movement centered in Kentucky, but exerted considerable influence in Tennessee and Indiana. In **The Christian Messenger,** which Stone began publishing in 1826, he deplored the sectarianism around them. [4] He wrote:

"The Christians of old were called a sect, while they were laboring to teach and live the religion of their Lord, and to discountenance and oppose every thing contrary to his revealed will. But a true church of Christ never was, and never can be, **voluntarily** a sect from the body of Christ; for this is contrary to the nature and laws of his kingdom. Had we voluntarily separated from the body of Christ, and formed ourselves into a distinct church, governed by laws of our own making; and should we reject a Christian, because he could not receive and be governed by our laws, then we might be called a sect in the worst sense of the word." [5]

In the meantime, the mantle of leadership had passed to Alexander Campbell. He was preaching up and down the Ohio River, engaging in religious debates designed to focus attention on their efforts, and publishing the **Christian Baptist.** In this paper he castigated sectarianism and called men to abandon it. Campbell's relationship with the Baptists began because of common views regarding baptism, both he and they believing that only immersion is sanctioned by Scripture. But in other areas there were fundamental differences. In his debate with John Walker in 1820 Campbell for the first time set forth his understanding of baptism for the remission of sins. In 1827 Walter Scott put into practice Campbell's teaching and began publicly proclaiming baptism for this purpose. Soon a great revival swept Ohio's Western Reserve.

The year 1831 marked the beginning of the fusion of the Stone and Campbell forces. The two efforts often found themselves in the same communities. The basic principles for which each stood were the same, and while there were differences of emphasis and some doctrinal disagreements, such as those relating to the purpose of baptism and the nature of God, there was enough in common to call for an effort at union. Actually, the two groups had been in communication for several years. An examination of Stone's **Christian Messenger** and Campbell's **Christian Baptist** reveals extensive discussion and correspondence. A meeting of the Stone "Christians" and the Campbell "Reformers" was called at Georgetown, Kentucky, on Christmas, 1831. At this historic meeting those present agreed to work for the union of their forces in the common cause of apostolic Christianity. Without any formal ecclesiastical action being taken (none was possible among autonomous congregations), but with considerable effort on the part of such men as Stone, John Rogers, John T. Johnson, and John Smith, unity was effected and within a short time they were in fact one body.

Until about the time of their merger, the Stone and Campbell forces were movements cutting across denominational lines, calling followers of Jesus from sectarianism to New Testament Christianity. This was especially true of those associated with Campbell. But now several factors caused an isolation from their religious neighbors. First, their emphasis on immersion for the remission of sins marked them as a people with a message that not all would accept. Second, an increasing awareness of what they stood for prompted denominational churches to shut their doors against them. Third, the fusion of forces doubled their numbers and served to further separate them from their religious neighbors. Whitley expresses the view that the 1830's were the first decade of a separate existence for those in the Restoration Movement and is probably correct in his assessment. [6]

The question must be raised as to what these people were at this point. Having protested against sectarianism, they now found themselves detached from their neighbors. Were they also a sect? Joseph Franklin described their condition in this way:

"The Disciples belonging to the Current Reformation are a separate people, not because they are hedged in by any denominational organization of their own, but because they are fenced out by the organizations of other professed Christians." [7]

A fuller and searching examination of their dilemma is considered by J. W. Roberts:

"Now we must ask in all candor . . . . What was the status of those new churches which took this stand at the first quarter of the 19th century? Were they denominational at this stage? In one sense of the definition, they recognized that they were. They were a separate religious group, with common beliefs, designations, organizations, and hopes. But they insisted that in the traditional sense of a 'denomination' they were not. They judged that it took several things to make a denomination: it took a denominational hierarchy with control of the local churches and preachers; it took a creed, binding an 'official' interpretation of the Bible in terms of some system of theology upon the church; it took a system of 'official' or 'ministerial' training with denominational 'ordination' which could control the training and thinking of the preachers; it took a hierarchically controlled missionary or placement service which could offer the ministry which cooperated employment independent of the local churches and deny it to a large extent to those who did not. Each denomination was the result of a fixation or over-emphasis on some particular point of doctrine, organization, or method of work. In these characteristic features they insisted that they were not a denomination. Only in the sense that they were forced into a separate organization were they a denomination." [8]

It would be a mistake, however, to presume that these people at this point had thought through all of the ramifications of undenominational Christianity. Having just emerged from sectarianism, they were still exploring the various aspects of the apostolic teaching. Their "search for the ancient order of things" had not yet been completed, nor may we add, is it ever completed unless one presumes to have an absolute corner on truth. True restoration calls for a continuing examination of our positions lest our practices crystalize into traditions and our traditions degenerate into sectarianism.

Until recently those in all segments of the Restoration Movement have protested against sectarianism and denied that they themselves constituted a sect. This has been based on the reasoning of the early reformers which equated non-sectarian Christianity with doctrinal soundness. Since they rejected all creeds and went to the book for all their teaching, they believed that to subscribe to a human confession of faith was denominational, but to accept the Scriptures, one's sole authority was to be be doctrinally correct and therefore undenominational. When they called for those in the "sects" to leave those bodies to become unsectarian, they were simply asking them to accept the truth as taught in God's word.

This perspective has much to commend it if we do in fact have the truth. There is a vital relationship between truth and undenominational Christianity. However, the essence of sectarianism is the party spirit. One can be as partisan with the truth as with error. Historically some of the most sectarian bodies have been those who contended most loudly that they, and they alone, had the truth. It is our thesis that because the reformers did not recognize the emergence of the party spirit among themselves, the concept of undenominational Christianity in the Restoration Movement was not fully developed in the 1830's, 1840's, and 1850's. Alexander Campbell, as will be seen, did not himself appear to have a complete understanding of the principle. Some began to think in distinct denominational terms. D.S. Burnett, President of the American Christian Bible Society and one of the more influential preachers and writers of his time, spoke of "one of our sister denominations" in his Third Annual Address to the society in 1849. [9] Even Benjamin Franklin, whose undenominational views were later clear, was understood by his son and biographer to have the denominational idea during this period. [10]

Joseph Franklin, in speaking of this time, advances the view that a denominational concept was definitely emerging:

"But the denominational idea, after a time, and especially after the work had gathered in a considerable degree of wealth and social position, took possession of the minds of many who were engaged in the work of reformation. Many joined in the search for a suitable denominational epithet, and set their minds to contriving some plan of organization." [11]

It is appropriate here to focus upon the practicality of the twin objectives of the Nineteenth Century Reformation—Christian union and restoration. It was the conviction of the early reformers that Christian unity could be achieved solely upon the basis

54

of the restoration of apostolic Christianity. Both goals were constantly stressed in their teaching. The early success of the movement as evidenced by the large number of accessions from the denominational world and the merging of the Stone and Campbell forces seemed to bear out the validity of the premise. And in theory, may we not say that the only way to achieve lasting unity is upon God's terms as revealed in his book? A question, however, was whether the religious world would subscribe to the premise. It became increasingly evident that it would not. Sectarianism was deeply rooted and men would not easily abandon the security represented by the status quo. When these churches found themselves existing as a distinct fellowship in the 1830's they were faced with two choices described by J. W. Roberts:

"**The First Alternative.** The first choice was to insist further upon the conformity to the pattern of the New Testament and to continue the emphasis upon the restoration of the first-century Christianity. But it was clear that this meant the abandonment of unity among the Protestant churches. To achieve the restoration of New Testament Christianity meant that the churches must take a positive stand against denominationalism and the doctrines and practices in the realm of faith that do not have universal consensus as belonging to the pattern of New Testament faith. It meant following a separate course and bearing before the religious world continuing witness that undenominational Christianity was possible.

"This step is what happened to much of the Restoration Movement in the 1840's and 1850's, Alexander Campbell at this period actually abandoned the dream of a united protestantism . . . .

"**The Second Alternative.** The alternative to this continued emphasis on the Restoration was to adapt the movement into a denominational pattern and try to work for unity through cooperation in formal or organizational means such as the later Federal Council of Churches and the Ecumenical Movement. This meant the actual abandonment of the moorings with which the movement began and grew. But this was the course chosen by elements which have today produced the Disciples of Christ." [12]

It should not be inferred that everyone recognized the practical tension between Christian union and restoration. Many continued to stress both principles and some still do. But the dichotomy caused by the two opposing views given by Roberts was to be evident in divisions occuring in the nineteenth and twentieth centuries. Few realized this at the time. A clear understanding of the undenominational idea would have helped immensely in bringing the picture into focus. But, five decades after Barton W. Stone and Thomas Campbell issued their historic documents defining basic elements of undenominational Christianity, the concept was still not clearly developed in the minds of those calling for a return to the ancient order. True, they condemned sectarianism in others, especially as they equated it with doctrinal error. Few of those associated with the movement would acknowledge being sectarian, although some, including Alexander Campbell as will be noted, were willing to be considered denominational. But relationships with their religious neighbors caused at least some to think and speak of themselves in denominational terms. It remained for another generation to clearly think through the implications of being just Christians in a sectarian world.

## FOOTNOTES

1. John Rogers, **The Biography of Elder Barton Warren Stone** (Cincinnati: J. A. and U. P. James, 1847), p. 50.

2. Charles Alexander Young, **Historical Documents Advocating Christian Union** (Chicago: Christian Century, 1904), pp. 19-23.

3. **Ibid.**, pp. 107-113.

4. Barton W. Stone, "Partyism," **The Christian Messenger,** August, 1827.

5. Barton W. Stone, **The Christian Messenger,** December, 1827.

6. Oliver Read Whitley, **Trumpet Call of Reformation** (St. Louis: Bethany Press, 1959), p. 90.

7. Joseph Franklin and J. A. Headington, **The Life and Times of Benjamin Franklin** (St. Louis: John Burns, 1879), p. 321.

8. J. W. Roberts, "Is the Church of Christ a Sect?" **The Restoration Principle, Abilene Christian College Annual Bible Lectures, 1962** (Abilene, Texas: ACC Students Exchange, 1962), pp. 169, 170.

9. Franklin and Headington, **Op. cit.,** p. 324.

10. **Ibid.**, p. 321.

11. **Ibid.**, p. 321.

12. J. W. Roberts, **Op. cit.**, pp. 170-174.

# CHAPTER 5
# ALEXANDER CAMPBELL AND SECTARIANISM

The Reformation of the Nineteenth Century resulted from the confluence of two streams of thought to which were added other lesser known tributaries. Movements are made by men and the thinking of these men inevitably shapes the direction of the movements. It is unfortunate that Barton W. Stone's influence in the development of the Restoration Movement has never been properly recognized. Yet, it is also true that Alexander Campbell's influence after the fusion of the Stone and Campbell forces was far greater than that of Stone. Not only did he live much longer, but he had greater intellectual impact.

Campbell's strength lay in his ability to grasp eminent principles and then to apply them. The concept of the "restoration of the ancient order" is an example. Moreover, he was a leader of leaders. Through his writing and speaking he influenced the common man and, more importantly, those leaders who would carry the principles for which he stood to places where he could not go. In effect, therefore, the thinking of Campbell shaped the concepts of the reformation.

Men were slow to take exception to Campbell. When the "sage of Bethany" had his Lunenburg correspondence quoted a few years before his death in the controversy over who might partake of the communion, it was with a ring of authority which those on the other side could not lightly disregard. On the other hand, it should not be assumed that others automatically agreed with Campbell. They had been too well schooled in the importance of following "The Book" to accept his views unquestioningly. Men like Jacob Creath, Jr., were not afraid to take him to task in controversies such as that pertaining to missionary societies.

Campbell, like every thinking person, changed his views through the years. Sometimes, as in the society controversy, he seemed unwilling to acknowledge that he had altered his position. Perhaps he was unaware that he had, but from time to time his critics would not hesitate to quote his earlier writings. On other themes he seems to have intentionally withheld his opinions until the opportune time. His expression of views in the "Lunenberg Letter" is a case in point. In defending himself against the charge of changing his stance and giving comfort to the sects, Campbell cited his earlier statements to prove that he had not changed. Yet it is also apparent that many had not previously understood his position and felt that he no longer believed as formerly on the question of "Christians among the sects." [1]

Because of his tremendous influence on others, an examination of Campbell's thinking on sectarianism and denominationalism is valuable. Beginning with the February 7, 1825, issue of the **Christian Baptist,** Campbell wrote a series of thirty articles extending over several years on "A Restoration of the Ancient Order of Things." In these articles he frequently condemned sectarianism. Typical is this early statement:

"But what kind of reformation is requisite to this end? It is not the erection of a new sect, the inventing of new shibboleths, or the setting up of a new creed, nor the adopting of any in existence save the New Testament, in the form in which it pleased the Spirit of God to give it. It is to receive it as it stands, and to make it its own interpreter, according to the ordinary rules of interpreting all books. It is not to go back to primitive Calvinism, or primitive Methodism, or primitive Lutheranism, but to primitive Christianity. The history of the church for many centuries proved, the history of every sect convinces us, that it is impossible for any one sect to gain such an ascendance as to embrace as converts the others and thus unite in one grand phalanx the christians against the allied powers of darkness, as it is to create a world. Every sect, with a human creed, carries in it, as the human body the seeds of its own mortality . . . . Where are the hundreds of sects that have already existed? They only live in history as beacons to posterity." [2]

Campbell felt it was his mission to call disciples out of the sects. This implied, of course, that there were Christians in sectarian groups. He wrote:

"I have no idea of seeing, nor one wish to see the sects unite in one grand army. This would be dangerous to our liberties and laws. For this the Savior did not pray. It is only the disciples of Christ dispersed amongst them, that reason and benevolence would call out of them. Let them unite who love the Lord, and then we shall soon see the hireling priesthood and their worldly establishments prostrate in the dust." [3]

To understand Campbell's views on sectarianism we need to appreciate his thinking relating to the nature of the church. He conceived of the universal body as being made up of all the saved:

"The **true** Christian church, or house of God, is composed of all those in every place that do publicly acknowledge Jesus of Nazareth as the true Messiah, and the only Saviour of men; and, building themselves upon the foundation of the Apostles and Prophets, associate under the constitution which he himself has granted and authorized in the New Testament, and are walking in his ordinances and commandments—and of none else." [4]

Campbell also thought of the universal church as composed of individual congregations. Thus, the universal church could operate when congregations banded together for common action. It was through this type of reasoning that he justified the missionary society. Two quotations, made twenty years apart, illustrate his views:

"The church, viewed in this light, is not one congregation or assembly, but the congregation of Christ, composed of all the individual congregations on earth. In this work of conversion the whole church by natural necessity, as well as by the authority of the great king, must cooperate." [5]

"Hence, there is but one kingdom of Christ, one body of Christ, or one church of Christ on earth. The word church, by reference to its occurrences in the New Testament, indicates the whole Christian community on earth . . . . Every individual church on earth stands to the whole church of Christ as one individual man to one particular church." [6]

Campbell's view of sectarianism was determined by his understanding of the biblical teaching on the subject. He went to the

Greek word, "hairesis," variously translated as heresy or sect, and established that in its basic import it means a separated party. He concluded that in Acts the implication of the word is essentially neutral. In that book, he declared:

"The term has nothing in it either reproachful or honorable—nothing virtuous or vicious. Hence it is equally applied to Pharisees, Sadducess, Nazarenes, or Christians, without any insinuation as to the character of the party." [7]

On the other hand, he determined that in the epistles the word always has a bad connotation. In this sense it is equivalent to faction. He thus divorced from the word the idea of error and concluded:

"Hence that ecclesiastical definition, viz.: '**Heresy denotes some erroneous opinion, tenet, or doctrine obstinately persisted in,**' is without any countenance from the New Testament." [8]

In Campbell's mind, however, there was a relationship between false teaching and sectarianism. In an article relative to the Baptists he stated:

"A sect, as we both view it, is a section or a party of a community, whether in philosophy, politics or religion. It is founded on some peculiar or distinctive theory, tenet, or interest, which is not catholic or universal . . . . Now, my dear sir, whatever society baptizes into this faith (that Jesus is the Christ) and builds the church upon it, is catholic; and whatever society does not, but substitutes for it any human opinion, speculation or experience, is, necessarily, sectarian. And he that defends these addenda and preaches them as necessary either to salvation or church fellowship is a fully developed sectarian—a heretic, in its original import...." [9]

Thus, Campbell believed that when one teaches religious error he becomes sectarian because by his teaching he has separated himself from those who occupy the universal ground. He concluded:

"So true it is that all strifes, contentions, parties, and sects grow out of corruption. Sects are the egress of corruptions." [10]

But, was there danger that Campbell and his co-workers might establish a new sect? He felt the possibility existed if one departed from the original apostolic ground:

"Finally, while endeavoring to abolish the old sects, let us be cautious that we do not form a new one. This may be done by either adding to, or subtracting from, the apostolic constitution a single item. Our platform must be as long and as broad as the New Testament. Every person that the Apostles would receive, if present, we must receive; and therefore the one faith, one Lord, one baptism, one hope, one body, one Spirit, one God and Father of all, must be made the reason of one, and only one, table....

"Every party in Christendom, without respect to any of its tenets, opinions, or practices, is a **heresy,** a schism—unless there be such a party as stands exactly upon the Apostles' ground." [11]

From these quotations it is apparent that Campbell thought of sectarianism in direct relation to truth and error. But he does not seem to have considered another question: is it possible for one to become sectarian with the truth? Cannot one possess sectarian attitudes without abandoning the basic tenets of apostolic Christianity? Does not sectarianism involve partisan attitudes as well as factional doctrines? Is it not possible for a group of Christians standing upon "the Apostles' ground" to exclude from their association others who are equally as correct in point of doctrine? And if they do so, do they not partake of the spirit of sectarianism? Undenominational Christianity cannot be considered apart from these questions and it does not appear that Campbell came to grips with them.

In 1855 Campbell published a letter which had been written to him twenty years earlier by John Waller who, in the intervening years, had embraced the principles espoused by Campbell. Waller's accusation and Campbell's reply reveal Campbell's thinking. Waller wrote:

"At the commencement of your career, you lectured much upon the pernicious effects of sectarianism. Your object, you said, was to destroy it. It was a noble design—a laudable pursuit. Long have pious persons prayed for the time when Christians should see eye to eye. But have you succeeded? Has the monster fallen? Are there fewer sects? Nay, is there not a new sect, composed of yourselves? Start not, my friend. I hope to show you that you are as much characterized by sectarian principles as others.

"What, then, do we understand by the word 'sect'? It literally imports separated and means in the acceptation applied to religious persons, a body of people distinct, by some peculiarities, from others, so that they may be distinguished and known by an appropriate name. Are you not a separate body? Are you not united and distinct from others? Have you not characteristic traits?" [12]

Campbell replied to the charge as follows:

"If we are a sect, then, we ask, In the day of judgment at whose door will this sin lie? The first Christians were a sect amongst the Jews. But on which party does the guilt lie!! The Christians, or those who made them a sect? . . . 'Are you not a separate body?' they say. Grant it. But who separated us? Did we excommunicate the Baptists or did they excommunicate us? . . . You made us a sect for cherishing catholic principles. And as certain as the Bible is true, you will be held guilty for it. You excommunicated us, not we you . . . . We are a sect—(shame upon our contemporaries!)—I say we are a sect by their exclusion of catholic principles. We have not a known article in our faith that is not as broad as Christendom, or more catholic than ever was Greek, or Roman, or Protestant denominational catholicism, dead or living." [13]

Thus Campbell was willing to accept the term sect in the neutral sense of a group apart, but at the same time he denied responsibility for that separation. It is perhaps in this sense that he was also willing to apply the word denomination to those in his association—a people separate from others and thus "denominated." He writes:

"I may add, in further corroboration of our anti-sectarian character and feelings now, that under the blessing of Heaven, a very large party has been formed, in many regions equalling any other denomination; and in others, where we have had an equal ratio of preachers, surpassing them in numbers; we as a **denomination** (emphasis—M. H.) are as desirous as ever to unite and co-operate with all Christians on the broad and vital principles of the New and everlasting Covenant." [14]

It is apparent that Campbell made a distinction between sectarianism, as he ordinarily used the term, and denominationalism. His distinction was not the sociological distinction sometimes made today. One is struck, as he reads the controversial discussions of this period, with the fact that men frequently fail to understand one another because of attaching different definitions to their words. To many then, as well as today, sectarianism and denominationalism were synonymous. Sixty-two years after Campbell made this statement the editor of the

64

**Millennial Harbinger Abridged** commented on Campbell's statement:

"If the word 'denomination' is accepted as a synonym for 'sect' and is taken to indicate that we have taken our place simply as one of the many denominations or sects of Christianity—we protest against being called a denomination—we prefer to be considered as a movement in the church pleading for the union of all who love our Lord, by a return to the faith and practice of the New Testament church. Our people have not followed Mr. Campbell in using this word: we feel that it is an offensive word as applied to our movement. The Disciples of Christ can not consent to become a denomination until we consent to degenerate into a sect." [15]

In summary, Campbell correctly conceived of the church as being comprised of all of the redeemed throughout the world. He definitely believed that there were Christians among the sects and he called them to leave such parties. His primary opposition to sectarianism was that when doctrinal error is taught it creates a separate party or sect. His equation of sectarianism and error is shared by many today and is probably true so far as it goes. But Campbell did not grapple with the problem of sectarian attitudes, as evident at Corinth, in the same way that he did with doctrinal error. A completely developed concept of undenominational Christianity, at least so far as its implications were concerned for those in the Restoration Movement, is not apparent. It remained for others after his death to seek a fuller restoration of that element of primitive Christianity.

## FOOTNOTES

1. Alexander Campbell, "Any Christians Among the Sects?", **Millennial Harbinger,** December, 1837, pp. 561, 562.

2. Alexander Campbell, "The Conversion of the World," **Christain Baptist,** January 5, 1824.

3. Alexander Campbell, "A Restoration of the Ancient Order of Things," **Christian Baptist,** April 4, 1825.

4. Alexander Campbell, **The Christian System** (Cincinnati: Standard Publishing), p. 55.

5. Alexander Campbell, **Millennial Harbinger,** July, 1834, p. 315.

6. Alexander Campbell, "Church Organization," **Millennial Harbinger,** June, 1853, p. 303.

7. Alexander Campbell, **The Christian System,** p. 77.

8. **Ibid.,** p. 79.

9. Alexander Campbell, "Are the Baptists a Sect?," **Millennial Harbinger,** September, 1851, pp. 522, 523.

10. Alexander Campbell, **The Christian System,** p. 80.

11. **Ibid.,** p. 84.

12. John L. Waller, "Letter to a Reformer, Alias Campbellite," written December 18, 1834, **Millennial Harbinger,** November, 1855, p. 616.

13. Alexander Campbell, "Letter to a Reformer, Alias Campbellite," **Millennial Harbinger,** November, 1855, pp. 619, 620.

14. Alexander Campbell, **Millennial Harbinger,** December, 1840.

15. Benjamin Lyon Smith, **The Millennial Harbinger Abridged** (Cincinnati: Standard Publishing, 1902), Vol. 2, p. 548.

# CHAPTER 6
# THE DEVELOPMENT
# OF A CONCEPT

"Are **we** a denomination?" This question, often asked in restoration history, has been answered in different ways. Essential to any response is one's definition of "denomination." Equally important is whom one is contemplating when he speaks of "we." In this chapter we will examine some of the early answers given to the query, and then notice the conclusions of those who seem to have most fully grasped the principle of undenominational Christianity.

In **Lard's Quarterly** of March, 1864, the third issue of the publication, Moses E. Lard addressed himself to the question, "Have we not become a sect?" In his article he declared that "sects exist not without the church but wholly within it." He viewed religious denominations not as sects, but as apostasies, though he acknowledged the presence of Christians within such groups. In response to the question he had asked, Lard concluded that those connected with the restoration effort did not intend to form a sect, did not intend to modify an existing one, but strove for the restoration of primitive Christianity. He observed that since no doctrine unsanctioned by the Bible had been introduced, and this is the basis by which a sect is measured, the charge of sectarianism in the Restoration Movement was without foundation. [1]

Neverthless, the following decades were to see considerable discussion of this question, "Are we a denomination?" An unknown writer in the **Millennial Harbinger** in the same year that Lard made his observations issued a warning:

"But now—we have become a 'Religious Body.' We have our shibboleths, our 'fixed principles,' and there is danger lest we, too, shall become infatuated with the Romish conceit of infallibility, against which we said so much in those early pioneer days, which the veterans among us have so much reason to remember." [2]

In 1870, the last year of its publication and a few years after the death of Alexander Campbell, W. K. Pendleton struck a sensitive nerve in the **Millennial Harbinger** in an article entitled, "What Is Sectarianism?" He wrote:

"It is charged by many that we are a sect. Is this so? . . . I believe we are all honestly against the thing in name,—I am not so sure that we are equally against it in fact. Let us understand ourselves, and seek also to enlighten our neighbors." [3]

Pendleton then called upon three leading religious publications in the Restoration Movement to respond to his question. These were the **American Christian Review,** the **Christian Standard,** and the **Apostolic Times.** Only Benjamin Franklin in his **Review** accepted the challenge. Pendleton had posed three specific questions and Franklin addressed himself to each. First, "What is sectarianism?" Franklin responded that a sect is a faction split off the main body and to be the cause of such schism is a great sin. Sectarianism, he contended, consists of the theories and tenets that produce schism, and when applied to the church, schism in the body. A sectarian is one who possesses theories and principles that tend to divide Christians.

Pendleton's second question was, "Are we a sect?" Franklin showed a grasp of the undenominational principle in his response:

"These Disciples of Christ, or Christians, claim to be members of the body of Christ—to belong to no other body. We may not know, and doubtless do not, in all cases, who or how many precisely are included in the general body. It, however, includes the whole family, the entire number of the redeemed—all the children of God. Defining the word 'we', then, as used by President Pendleton, as meaning the children of God in the aggregate, or the body of Christ, we deny that we are a sect." [4]

Note that Franklin equated the church, not with a specific brotherhood of which he was a part, but rather with the body of Christ embracing all of the saved, as God, not we, makes the determination. Quite correctly he concluded that this body is not a sect.

The third question of Pendleton was, "Are there sectarians holding prominent and representative positions among us?" In this he was focusing on sectarianism within the Lord's body. Here Franklin expressed grave concern.

"There are two elements in our midst, entirely alien to each other, at war, as much as flesh and spirit, in Paul's description. Some are clearly drifting into one current, and some into the other. The different things in which they manifest themselves, at one time in this and then in that, are not the cause, but only the occasion for the manifestation. These two elements have existed fifteen years or more, but their growth has been continuous, and is increasing of late." [5]

Franklin's observation was prophetic. Within twenty years of his writing the Restoration Movement was to be fractured into two groups, although even in 1890 this fact was not universally recognized. Superficially the cause of the division was disagreement over instrumental music in worship. And this was vitally important since it involved worship and the interrelation of Christians. Yet it should be noted that when Franklin made his observation few churches had introduced the instrument and fifteen years earlier, which he marks as the approximate beginning of the separation, none had. Of course, the question of the validity of the missionary society which was a major factor in the division was then being hotly argued. But in retrospect, we can now see that there were differences in attitudes and emphasis which were even more fundamental.

It soon became apparent that there were conflicting views on how the Bible should be interpreted. It is in this period that the stress between the twin objectives of Christian union and restoration begins to become evident. While most people probably continued to feel that practically speaking both were compatible, some neglected the Christian union emphasis while stressing restoration, while others gave less and less importance to restoration while striving for religious union.

There is another factor that gradually began to emerge. This related to the concept of the church. An increasing number began to think of God's people in denominational terms. Others, such as Franklin, were striving for a clear understanding of the nature of the New Testament church. This was doubtless (at least partially) what Franklin had in mind when he responded as he did to Pendleton's question about "sectarians among us."

Early in 1878 Isaac Errett, editor of **Christian Standard,** reprinted an article by F. G. Allen which had been run in the **Apostolic Times.** In an editorial entitled "Are We a Denomination?" Errett responded that there is a difference between a sect and a denomination, and that in the accepted sense those of the Restoration Movement constituted a denomination because they were "a class or collection of individuals called by the same name." [6] Two weeks later an article by W. W. Hayden in the same paper reasoned:

"Our denominational status is a question of fact, not of definition or causes. Are we a body of religious people separate and distinct from other bodies of religious people? Certainly we are." [7]

Hayden further argued that whether **we** are a denomination depends on one's point of view. He concluded that factually speaking the Restoration Movement was a denomination. It was in this same vein that J. H. Garrison concluded:

"Sometime ago there was a controversy between some of our papers on the question: 'Are we a denomination?' It occurs to us that there is another question lying behind that, that will help to answer it. It is this: Are we a church? If so, we are certainly a denominational church like all the rest." [8]

Garrison did not answer the question he posed, but observed that the reformers did not intend to form a denomination and that sectarianism is certainly wrong. However, the comments of Errett, Hayden, and Garrison all focus on the attitude of the world in general toward the Restoration Movement, namely, that because those composing it were a distinct people, they constituted a denomination.

It should be observed that in spite of efforts of undenominational disciples of Christ to set forth their plea to be just Christians, some in the religious world will always regard them as sectarian. This is true regardless of the century or the land in which such an effort takes place. The world insists on "pigeon-holing" those it does not understand. Does it follow, however, that one must accept denominational status simply because of the attitude of others? What really was emerging in some people in the last part of the nineteenth century in the Restoration Movement was the willing acceptance of denominational status because of their inability to communicate a non-sectarian position to the religious world. One major reason that such a view could not be communicated was that they themselves did not clearly understand what is involved in undenominational Christianity.

In the intervening years the same questions have been raised many times in various segments of the Restoration Movement. In the February 1, 1902, issue of the **Christian Standard,** Marion Stevenson in a front page article asked the same question Isaac Errett had raised twenty-four years before in the same paper, "Are we a denomination?" Stevenson's response was negative; interesting in light of Errett's positive answer earlier. [9]

Equally intriguing is the attitude of the **Christian Evangelist** which by the 1930's and 1940's had become the liberal voice in the movement. In 1947 the publication vehemently rejected denominational status for the Disciples of Christ:

"It is amazing to hear the accusation that Disciples of Christ are tending toward denominationalism. That is the last frenzy of the religious introvert. There is no more likelihood the Disciples of Christ will accept a denominational status than that the United States will become a monarchy." [10]

Yet, in spite of the protestations of the 1947 **Christian Evangelist,** an editorial in the same paper ten years earlier had taken an opposing position:

"The Disciples of Christ, as everyone acquainted with our history knows, came into being largely as a protest movement against the divided state of Christendom. It was never the intention of the fathers of this movement to organize a new denomination, their contention being that they were merely forming an association of Christians desirous of healing the breach within the church. To this day the word 'denomination', when applied to the Disciples of Christ, is deeply resented by hosts of our members. The word 'communion' we will tolerate, but not 'denomination', for this, we protest, we are not.

"And yet today the rest of the Christian world views the Disciples of Christ as a denomination among denominations. If they use the word 'communion' rather than 'denomination' when speaking of us it is out of courtesy and not because they believe us to occupy any different status from that occupied by other recognized religious bodies.

71

"And must we not candidly admit that we have most, if not all, of the earmarks of a denomination? We are a separate people, requiring our members to come out of the other religious bodies if they would join us. We have our own separate corporate existence with conventions, boards, officers, and secretaries. We maintain separate and distinct missionary, educational, and benevolent enterprises. We have our own press and our own Sunday school literature. Even more, a host of our members possess as strong a 'denominational mind' as do any Baptists, Methodists, or Presbyterians. Whether we like it or not the years have seen us driven increasingly away from Thomas Campbell's concept of a 'Christian Association' and in the direction of an out-and-out denomination." [11]

Perhaps the best analysis of attitudes toward denominationalism in the liberal wing of the Restoration Movement in recent years is found in the 1948 "Commission on Restudy of the Disciples of Christ." This commission was appointed by the international convention of the Disciples and was made up of people of widely differing views. Its evaluation is an attempt to bring into perspective the assorted attitudes held at the time of the study. In a section entitled, "A Denomination or Movement?" the commission draws the following conclusions:

"It is agreed that in our inception we were a movement rather than a denomination; that historically we have endeavored to avoid denominational status; and that to be content with occupying a status as one among many denominations is to abandon our attempt to realize unsectarian Christianity.

"Some of us hold that we must therefore refuse to accept any denominational status, and rather seek to occupy non-partisan and ultimate ground in all points of faith and order.

"Others hold that we are compelled by the existing order of Protestant denominationalism to be a denomination, while at the same time testifying against denominationalism and exploring all possibilities of finding common ground on which all Christians may stand.

"Still others, in the judgment of this commission few in number, hold that we have in the processes of history become a denomination, possessing peculiarities and identity in a manner similar to the denominations round about us." [12]

As to the factors causing these divergent points of view, the commission continues:

"Our study of the history and ideals of our people has led us to the conclusion that a basic cause of our division and our more serious dissensions, both past and present, lies in a difference of understanding with respect to the fundamental purpose of our movement.

"Our commission agrees that the two concepts of unity and restoration have been from the beginning held together in a parity of mutual dependence .... During the past half century, however, in the thinking of a considerable section of our people the ideals of union and restoration have tended to fall apart as two concepts that are not co-ordinate or mutually dependent ....

"Some among us maintain that these two conceptions of union and restoration must be held together .... Others among us are content to abandon the concept of the restoration of the primitive church and center our emphasis upon union .... Still others believe that a new synthesis of these two concepts of unity and restoration is possible." [13]

In the twenty-five years since the commission was set up division has become a reality among those congregations in the Restoration Movement using the instrument in worship. The more liberal group, the Disciples of Christ, has restructured, partially abandoning congregational autonomy. They are seeking to fulfill the ideal of union expressed by Hampton Adams, "a denomination that hopes to die . . . in order that they may live more fully in the universal church of the Lord Jesus Christ." [14] As such they have accepted denominational status and have engaged in discussions with the Council on Christian Union (COCU) pursuing a merger with other religious bodies, including several which are non-immersionist. The restoration concept, at least so far as understood in the early days of the movement, has been abandoned by them in the interest of union. This union, if ever achieved, will be denominational in its scope and undenominational Christianity will not be a part of it.

The more conservative element of the instrumental churches, sometimes known as "independents" and congregationally called either Christian Churches or churches of Christ, generally accepts the plea for undenominational Christianity as valid. Their cleavage with the Disciples is nearly complete. The differences are basic and relate to the fundamental principles of restoration as set forth in the early part of the Restoration Movement. A directory of congregations and church workers published among these people is entitled, **"Directory of the Ministry of the Un-**

denominational Fellowship of Christian Churches and Churches of Christ." [15]

Among the most conservative congregations of the Restoration Movement there has never been an abandonment of the undenominational plea, except perhaps on the part of a few individuals in recent years. Occasionally one will read a statement such as the following:

"All our protestations to the contrary notwithstanding, **we are a denomination.** We should confess it and join other denominational Christians in asking God's forgiveness and His guidance." [16]

Yet this statement is highly atypical and whether the above charge is true or false, these churches have never acknowledged a denominational position.

The **Gospel Advocate**, which became the most influential publication among convervative congregations during the period of the separation, stressed the non-sectarian concept. From 1890 to 1900 F. D. Srygley was one of the editors. H. Leo Boles says of him:

"He studied the church from every angle as revealed in the New Testament. He wrote much about it, and no one of his day, and probably no one since his time, had a clearer conception of the New Testament church and its mission than did F. D. Srygley." [17]

An example of Srygley's insight is found in this statement:

"The sum of it all is that the church of God is one spiritual body in Christ, in which every Christian is a member. No one can become a Christian without also becoming at the same time and by the same process, a member of the spiritual body of Christ." [18]

Over and over again Srygley stressed the undenominational principle. He did not apologize for his constant repetition. He said, "To hammer constantly on one point is both tedious and monotonous, but no man can drill a hole in a hard substance without hitting many licks in the same place."

There were others whose understanding of the biblical view of the church was clear and who in turn influenced still others. F. G. Allen, Joseph Franklin, M. C. Kurfees, G. C. Brewer, and J.N.

Armstrong are five men worthy of special note. It is unfortunate that the emphasis on undenominational Christianity has been less in recent years than during the time of F. D. Srygley and his contemporaries. True, words such as undenominational and non-sectarian are frequently heard, but as will be observed, often their meaning is not understood. There is too much of a "practice gap" among all the segments of the Restoration Movement that still profess to be **Christians only**. The great need is for a reexamination of the exact nature of the New Testament church.

Having considered the development of various attitudes in the Restoration Movement, attention should be given to the teachings of those who most fully grasped the undenominational principle. Perhaps by examining the understanding of those of another generation we can better appreciate what it means to be just a Christian.

Elijah Goodwin, who died in 1879, was one of the first generation of restoration preachers and an editor for many years. He used a hypothetical illustration to demonstrate how a simple apostolic church might be established.

"Should a company of persons who never saw a Bible or a priest be shipwrecked, and cast upon some uninhabited island; should they there find a Bible containing both Testaments, and, by reading it, they all become firm believers in Christ, the Son of God, and the divine Saviour—suppose, then, that one of the company baptizes one of the number, and he, in turn, baptizes the rest; suppose, then, that they adopt that holy Book, containing the teaching of the apostles and prophets of God, as their only rule of faith and practice; they appoint their bishops and deacons according to that Book, and proceed to keep the ordinances as they were delivered by the apostles—that would be, to all intents and purposes, the same body of people—not the same persons, but the same religious organism. It would be the regular, pure and holy apostolic church." [19]

One of the most lucid writers on the undenominational theme was Frank G. Allen, editor of **The Old Path Guide** about 1880, who frequently examined the subject. Reference has already been made to the emphasis given by F. D. Srygley to undenominational Christianity. He was an early associate of Allen in publishing **The Old Path Guide** and one wonders to what extent Allen, twenty years his senior, may have influenced Srygley in his thinking. The following lengthy quotation from Allen is given because it is one of the best expositions on the subject known to the writer:

"(1). Our plea for Christian union implies that there are Christians to unite.

"It has ever been admitted that God has children among the denominations—those who have obeyed the Gospel and are serving Him in the spirit of humility. To deny that there are Christians apart from those who stand identified with us in our work of restoration, would be to make our plea for Christian union both meaningless and senseless. While we believe that many identified with the denominations are Christians, they have taken on much that is neither Christianity nor any part of it; and this we labor to have them put away. These are the things that cause sectarian divisions, with all their evils. Such people are more than Christians; and what they have in addition is wrong. In being more than Christians they become less than what Christians should be. This may appear paradoxical, but it is true.

"It will be seen, therefore, that while we claim to be Christians only, we do not claim to be the only Christians. Our principles will not allow us to be anything else; and we strive to have others satisfied with being the same. Hence the charge so often made, that we arrogate to ourselves alone the name Christian, is false. We simply decline to be more than this, because God's people in New Testament times were nothing more. To those who love the simplicity of apostolic Christianity this position will commend itself with great force.

"(2). Our plea for the union of God's people implies that the Church of God includes more than those engaged in this work of restoration. In other words, that the Church of God is a more comprehensive term than those descriptive of our work.

"God's church is composed of individual Christians, wherever they may be. Of His Church they become members by obedience to the Gospel. They do not forfeit their membership in God's Church till they cease to be His children. As long as they are children of God they are members of the body of Christ. Hence if there are children of God outside of what the world calls Camp-bellism, the Church of God extends beyond the same boundary. Consequently, while we claim to belong to the Church of God only, we do not claim to be the only people who belong to the Church of God. Others who belong to the Church of God also belong to a church **not** of God. They belong to **two** churches, while we belong to but one. Hence the whole charge of exclusiveness brought against us on this point turns on the question as to whether or not it is one's privilege to belong to but **one** church, and that the Church of God. That God's people in ancient times belonged to but one Church is simply an admitted fact; and His people now should belong to that, and that only, to which they belonged, then.

"In the New Testament the word **church** is applied to a local congregation and to the whole body of believers. It is never used in any denominational sense. Consequently we may not limit it to any religious people now, unless we believe that they include all God's children. While, therefore, we belong to the Church of God only, and our principles will not allow us to belong to any other, we should be careful to give to that term no mere denominational meaning. When I say I belong to the Church of God, the Church of Christ, or any other scriptural term by which the same thing is designated, I mean that I belong to God's redeemed family,

> 'Part of whom have crossed the flood,
> And part are crossing now.'

"(3). From this it follows that our work of restoration is wholly undenominational.

"When the Church of Christ shall be restored as it was at the beginning, or to the extent of that restoration, it will be wholly undenominational. This is true from the simple fact that there were no denominations then. No one then belonged to the Church of God and also to some denomination. All the Apostles belonged to the Church of God. None of them belonged to any denomination. So of all the disciples. What was true then may be true now; and to the extent that this is true, or ever shall be true, in the restoration of the Church, to that extent will denominationalism cease. Our plea means its destruction. It can mean nothing less. This is the secret of their intense hatred of it. But be it so; truth can never compromise with error." [20]

Allen's statement that "while we claim to be Christians only, we do not claim to be the only Christians," was an oft repeated declaration of the reformers of that period. On the one hand it rejects denominationalism while disclaiming the idea that any group of people can circumscribe God's children on the basis of human determination. There is here a specific rejection of the complete equation of the church of God with the Restoration

Movement, or with any part of that movement. When Allen thought and spoke of the divine family he was not limiting it to those of his immediate association since he was incapable of knowing all of those who had the approval of the Lord. To him the body of Christ was composed of the saved as determined by Jesus himself. This was, and is, undenominational Christianity.

In 1920, M. C. Kurfees, also an earlier associate with F. G. Allen in **The Old Path Guide,** examined even more fully in the **Gospel Advocate** the condition of people in the religious denominations and their relationship to the unsectarian church of God:

"Without stopping here to discuss in detail the steps which, according to the New Testament, are essential to entrance into the church, we may observe that, while many persons in at least some of the denominations have not complied with all terms of admission and hence are not in the church, nevertheless, many others in the different denominations have complied with them and are, therefore, in spite of their erroneous practices otherwise, in, and are a part of, the church. The members constituting the different divisions or parties in the church at Corinth were, nevertheless, all in the church in spite of their erroneous teachings and practices, and in writing to them Paul addressed them all as 'the church of God which is at Corinth' (1 Corinthians 1:2, 2 Corinthians 1:1). Among them were Paulites, Cephasites, Apollosites, and those who were simply Christians, or who held to the name of Christ alone; yet Paul recognizes them all as being in, and a part of, the church of God at that place.

"Moreover, let it be distinctly observed just here that even those among them who rejected the names of Paul, Cephas, and of Apollos, and consistently held to the name of Christ alone, he did not address as 'the church of God which is at Corinth,' for the simple reason that they were not **'the** church,' but only a part of the church. The fact that they were not involved in error as were the others did not make them exclusively the church. The others, who were egregiously involved in error on some things and were sinning in being broken up into conflicting parties and divisons, were, nevertheless, in spite of their erroneous practices, a part of the church of God at Corinth; and hence, all of them of all the parties were addressed by the apostle as 'the church of God which is at Corinth.'

"In precisely the same way today, when persons do what God has commanded them to do for that purpose, they enter into, and become a part of, his church, and their unfortunate denominational entanglement in error on other points in no wise affects this fact. This does not mean, nor does it imply, that persons among them who have not done what God has commanded for that purpose, but have merely complied with a substitute for it, are also in the church. No one can properly claim that persons are in the church of God unless they have complied with the terms which God himself has stipulated for that purpose, and not merely a substitute for them. But when they have complied with the identical terms stipulated by God for the purpose, they enter into, and become a part of, his church in spite of the fact that they may be involved in error and make mistakes on other points; and hence, in any attempt to consider or speak of the church of God in such a situation and environment, we are compelled, if we would speak as the Bible speaks, to recognize these facts in our speech. To refuse to recognize persons as being in the church of God, when they have complied with God's own terms of admission, merely because they make mistakes at other points, would make it proper to deny that any of us, who make mistakes in any way whatever, are in his church." [21]

Kurfees' observations lucidly expose our sectarian bias when we define the body of Christ according to our terms rather than the Lord's. We can greatly profit by reexamining the concepts of such men of God.

The restoration plea called for those Christians enmeshed in denominationalism to leave their sectarian association. Thus F. D. Srygley wrote:

"My understanding of the New Testament is that all Christians are in the church of God. The same thing that makes one a Christian constitutes him a member of the church. When Christians get into sects, parties, or denominations, they are in something more than the church of God. A Christian who belongs to the Baptist Church, for instance, is in the church of God and the Baptist Church both. The idea is to get him out of the Baptist Church and leave him in the church of God." [22]

Abstract ideas are often difficult to grasp. Undenominational Christianity is one of those abstractions. Beset as we are by a denominational system imposed upon us by generations of thought it is hard to perceive the possibility and the wisdom of being just Christians. It is so much easier to allow our thinking to be molded by the thought patterns of our religious neighbors. But we may be thankful that there have been those who have grappled with this grand conception, so simple in its expression and yet so difficult of execution.

# FOOTNOTES

1. Moses E. Lard, "Have We Not Become a Sect?", **Lard's Quarterly,** March, 1864, pp. 22-39.

2. Anonymous ("Senex"), "Free Discussion," **Millennial Harbinger,** March, 1864, p. 170.

3. W. K. Pendleton, "What Is Sectarianism?", **Millennial Harbinger,** April, 1870, p. 236.

4. Benjamin Franklin, "What Is Sectarianism?", **Millennial Harbinger,** June, 1870, p. 354.

5. **Ibid.,** p. 356.

6. Isaac Errett, "Are We a Denomination?", **Christian Standard,** January 26, 1878, p. 28.

7. W. W. Hayden, "Our Denominational Attitude," **Christian Standard,** February 16, 1878.

8. J. H. Garrison, "What Is Our Mission?", **The Christian,** July 15, 1880.

9. Marion Stevenson, "Are We a Denomination?", **Christian Standard,** February 1, 1902, p. 159.

10. "Conventions of the Free," **Christian Evangelist,** August 6, 1947, p. 763.

11. "The Dilemma of the Disciples," **Christian Evangelist,** March 11, 1937.

12. **The Report of the Commission on Restudy of the Disciples of Christ** (International Convention of the Disciples of Christ, 1948), p. 11.

13. **Ibid.,** p. 14.

14. Hampton Adams, **Why I am a Disciple of Christ** (New York: Thomas Nelson and Sons, 1957), p. 109.

15. **Directory of the Ministry of the Undenominational Fellowship of Christian Churches and Churches of Christ, 1973** (Springfield, Illinois: Directory of the Ministry, 1973.)

16. Logan Fox, "Destiny or Disease?", **Voices of Concern** (St. Louis: Mission Messenger, 1966), p. 30.

17. H. Leo Boles, **Biographical Sketches of Gospel Preachers** (Nashville: Gospel Advocate, 1932), pp. 428, 429.

18. F. D. Srygley, **The New Testament Church** (Nashville: McQuiddy Printing, 1910), p. 93.

19. Elijah Goodwin, "The Sect Everywhere Spoken Against," **New Testament Christianity** (Columbus, Indiana: Z. T. Sweeney, 1939), vol. 1, p. 58.

20. F. G. Allen, "Our Strength and Our Weakness," **New Testament Christianity**, vol. 2., pp. 244-247.

21. M. C. Kurfees, "Bible Things by Bible Names Further Considered," **Gospel Advocate,** September 2, 1920, p. 862.

22. F. D. Srygley, **Op. Cit.,** pp. 50, 51.

# CHAPTER 7
# "YOUR SPEECH BETRAYS YOU"

"I'm Church of Christ all the way," the newcomer informed me. I was visiting her following her phone call upon moving to our city. Perhaps I should have corrected her speech, but not wishing to offend before getting to know her better, I remained silent.

But I was disturbed. Some might think I would have rejoiced at such an affirmation of church loyalty. Surely, here was one who would never depart from the faith. I was disturbed, not only because the Christian lady's language was unbiblical, but because it betrayed a loyalty to a denomination rather than to Christ. Our Lord's church is not a denomination, but her conception of it was thoroughly sectarian. It was almost as if she had said, "I was born a Democrat, I have always been a Democrat, and I will die a Democrat. May the Democrats always be right, but my party right or wrong."

The body of Christ is comprised of all the saved throughout the world and should never be thought of in denominational terms. If we conceive of Christ's church as just another denomination, our Christian faith will remain stunted. We then hold no personal allegiance to Jesus Christ. Perhaps that is why the "Church-of-Christ-all-the-way" lady has worshipped with her fellow Christians only occasionally in the years she has been in our city. Sectarian loyalty is long on words, but may be short on practice.

In the Restoration Period of Israel following the Babylonian captivity, the Jewish leaders had difficulty in maintaining the doctrinal and moral integrity of the Jews. Much of the problem stemmed from Israel's contamination by her neighbors. The Jewish governor, Nehemiah, described the problem in this way: "In those days also I saw the Jews who had married women of Ashdod, Ammon, and Moab; and half of their children spoke the language of Ashdod, and they could not speak the language of Judah, but the language of each people" (Nehemiah 13:23, 24). The problem of the Jews was not the foreign speech itself, but the contaminated language was symptomatic of a deeper problem. If we, like the lady mentioned, are guilty of speaking the language of Ashdod, it is an indication of the imperfection of our concept of undenominational Christianity.

In the earliest days of the church the followers of Jesus were described simply as disciples, the term being used hundreds of times in the gospels. Other words designating God's people in the New Testament include **saints** (Romans 1:7), **brethren** (Colossians 1:2), **priests** (1 Peter 2:5,9), and **heirs** (Romans 8:17). But it was the term **Christian** by which Jesus' followers most commonly came to be known. We are first introduced to it in Acts 11:26. "And in Antioch the disciples were for the first time called Christians." Whether it was a nickname given by enemies or adopted by the disciples themselves is not here stated, but that it was accepted by them as a fitting term for a follower of Jesus is apparent. They were "Christ-ians," disciples of Christ.

The term **Christian** was evidently common some years later when King Agrippa informed Paul, "In a short time you think to make me a Christian!" (Acts 26:28) or as the passage is rendered in the more familiar King James Version, "Almost thou persuadest me to be a Christian." The only other New Testament use of the word is in 1 Peter 4:16 where the apostle declares, "Yet if one suffers as a Christian, let him not be ashamed, but under that name let him glorify God." In light of the universal usage of the word from the post-apostolic period forward, it may surprise us that it is found in only these three places in the New Testament. Nevertheless, that it is a divinely approved descriptive term for God's people cannot be doubted in light of the usages we do have.

When the apostolic church is viewed biblically we find it called by descriptive terms rather than a proper name. It is the **kingdom** (Hebrews 12:28), **the household of faith** (Galatians 6:10), **the household of God** (1 Timothy 3:15), the **body of Christ** (1 Corinthians 12:27), and **the way** (Acts 19:9,23). The latter term is used six times in Acts to describe the fellowship of the saints.

Of course, the most common designation of the divine body is **the ekklesia,** or **the church,** as the word is usually translated. The word properly means "the called out." As previously noted, its basic import is that of a gathering of citizens called out of their homes into an assembly. It is used in this sense in Acts 19:39 where we read "But if you seek anything further, it shall be settled in the regular assembly (ekklesia)." Even though Christians are called out of the world of darkness into the light of the son of God (1 Peter 2:9,10), it is questionable how much should be made of the etymology of the word as applied to Christ's church.

In several places the ownership of the church is indicated in the phrase employed. "Or do you despise the **church of God** and humiliate those who have nothing?" (1 Corinthians 11:22). "Take heed to yourselves and to all the flock, in which the Holy Spirit has made you guardians, to feed the **church of the Lord** which he obtained with his own blood" (Acts 20:28). In this passage "Lord" obviously refers to Christ. Again, "All the **churches of Christ** greet you" (Romans 16:16). Here church is found in the congregational sense and is plural. In these passages a proper name is not used, but possession is indicated. One might as accurately speak of "God's church," "the Lord's church," or "Christ's church."

One other passage should be noted. In Hebrews 12:23 we read of "the assembly (church) of the first-born who are enrolled in heaven." Although Jesus is the first-born from the dead (Colossians 1:18), in this instance **first-born** refers to those who make up the church, or Christians, rather than denoting ownership. This is shown by the plural use of the Greek word for **first-born**.

Summing the matter up, the society of the redeemed is described by various terms in the New Testament with **church** being used more frequently than any other word. Usually the church is not otherwise defined, but when it is, possession is ordinarily indicated. Never is the term used as a proper name nor is any proper name applied to the divine body in the New Testament.

A study of the terminology in the Restoration Movement will help us understand some of the difficulties faced by contemporary Christians in their effort to express themselves biblically. Those connected with Barton W. Stone were dubbed Newlights by their enemies, but they preferred to be called Christians. Because of their early association with the Baptists, those under the influence of the Campbells were called Reforming Baptists or simply Reformers while Campbellites was the nickname used by their enemies. Alexander Campbell preferred the term Disciples. After the fusion of the Stone and Campbell forces there was considerable discussion as to the most appropriate designation. Writing in 1879, Joseph Franklin puts the matter in focus:

"The principles of the Reformers were such as to cut them loose from all sectarian organizations; and, existing as separate people, there began to be felt a necessity for some distinctive denominational epithet. Regarding Alexander Campbell as the leader, the people around them soon resolved the difficulty by calling the Reformers, 'Campbellites,' while the aggregate of the churches were styled the 'Campbellite Church.' By the same authority the Kentucky Reformers were called 'Newlights' and their connection, the 'Newlight Church.'

"'Campbellite Church' and 'Newlight Church' was an easy and ready way of distinguishing the two peoples from each other and from the religious parties around them. But those who held with Mr. Campbell so persistently and so emphatically repudiated the term 'Campbellite,' that common courtesy has commanded the disuse of the term. 'Reform Church,' and 'Disciple Church,' have been used in some localities, but have never been acknowledged by the people themselves as appropriate. 'Christian Church' is, perhaps, most current of all terms used for this purpose, and withal the least objectionable to the people for whom a name is sought.

"The situation is one of considerable difficulty. Separated by our principles from the sects and parties of Christendom, we desire to speak of ourselves, or of 'our brotherhood,' as such. We want a Bible term, for we profess to be guided by the Bible in all things. But all terms in the Bible apply either to the local congregations, or to the whole body of Christians. There is no Bible name for 'our brotherhood,' in this sectarian sense. It would be well if all the members of the Churches of Christ would abandon the denominational idea altogether. There is an exclusiveness involved that is contradictory to the principles of the Reformation." [1]

The terms Campbellism and Campbellites were universally rejected by those to whom they were applied. Alexander Campbell early expressed his view, often repeated later:

"A correspondent in Kentucky asks me, 'What is Campbellism?' To which I answer—It is a nickname of reproach invented and adopted by those whose views, feelings, and desires are all sectarian—who cannot conceive of Christianity in any other light than an ism." [2]

Writing fifty years later F. G. Allen expressed the same view:

"The people who 'Philalethes' so 'courteously' calls Campbellites are not a denomination, and hence need no 'denominational title.' Were they a denomination they could not object to a denominational name. On the contrary, they simply claim to be Christians; to belong to the church of God; and thus stand identified with all God's children of every age and nation. While they claim to be Christians only, they do not claim that they only are Christians. They recognize God's people among the denominations, but they deplore the denominational names and divisions which keep them apart. What they condemn in others they cannot accept for themselves. Hence they can not in consistency accept any denominational title, be it Campbellite or Paulite." [3]

The dilemma of those in the Restoration Movement as well as their reaction to the response of their religious neighbors is clearly expressed by Joseph Franklin:

"The Disciples protested constantly, during the early years of the Reformation, that they were not a 'sect,' and that it was no part of their mission to attempt the formation of a new sectarian organization. How this could be, the religious parties already in existence, could not, or would not, understand. They persistently recognized a denomination which they called, 'The Campbellite Church,' and insisted that Alexander Campbell was its founder. [4] If the Reformers said, 'We are simply Disciples of Christ, and we belong only to the Church of Christ,' they were understood at once to use the term 'Church of Christ' in a limited or denominational sense, exactly equivalent to the term 'Campbellite Church,' as used by themselves. We have ... called attention to the fact that the Disciples began to feel embarrassed for the want of some unobjectionable term which would bear such an application, and that finally, 'Christian Church,' was currently used in that way." [5]

In practice "Church of Christ" and "Christian Church" were used interchangeably at the congregational level. "Disciples of Christ" was used less frequently to refer to the local church, although it was a common appellation to the movement as a whole. Some objected to "Christian Church" as unbiblical. As early as 1865 Moses E. Lard wrote:

"Suppose, now, that Christ has a church in a given place. How shall we appropriately designate it? Call it simply **the church of God, or the church of Christ.** These are Scriptural names; no others are. But it will be asked: What is the distinction between the expressions church of Christ and Christian church? I answer: that is Scriptural and always will be; this is not Scriptural and never will be. Purity of speech requires that we speak of Bible things in Bible language. Church of Christ is Bible language; Christian church is not." [6]

Many did not agree and Christian Church continued to be widely used. F. G. Allen objected to its use, not on biblical grounds, but because he saw in it a sectarian application. After arguing that it is as biblical to speak of the Christian Church as the Christian dispensation, Christian Scriptures, or Christian baptism, he adds:

"Our objection to the expression 'Christian Church,' comes from quite a different source. That is, from the fact, that there seems to be a growing disposition to use it exclusively in **a denominational** sense. It is now generally used to designate those only who stand identified with the Reformation inaugurated by the Campbells, Stone and others. We are justified in using the term only as the exact equivalent of 'the Church of Christ,' and we are not justified in limiting this broad, grand term to anything that is, in a popular sense, denominational. It is because of a disposition, therefore, to use the expression, 'Christian Church,' in a narrower sense than its equivalent—Church of Christ—is used in the New Testament, that we do not advocate its use. True, we may use 'Church of Christ' in what would be regarded as a denominational sense, and some do; but there is less tendency in that direction." [7]

Candor forces us to inquire if **Church of Christ** has not come to be used as denominationally today as **Christian Church** was when Allen wrote. F. D. Srygley, whose editorials in the **Gospel Advocate** from 1890 to 1900 constantly stressed the undenominational concept, rejected **Christian Church** as unbiblical, but spoke so frequently of "the church of Christ" as to cause us to wonder if others might not have read into his undenominational use of the phrase a denominational meaning.

J. H. Garrison, editor of **The Christian,** focused on the problem of terminology in a series of articles in 1880 entitled, "What Is Our Mission?"

"This fault into which most of us have fallen, of alluding to our brotherhood of co-workers in this reformation as 'the Christian Church,' or the 'Church of Christ,' as some prefer, is the result of carelessness of speech, for no one, perhaps, would affirm what the phrase naturally implies. Nevertheless, the constant usage of such phrases tend to foster wrong ideas, especially in the minds of the young, and to beget the very spirit which is a part of our mission to destroy—the sect spirit." [8]

Unfortunately, the Reformation of the Nineteenth Century has fragmented. The terms applied to local churches reflect both an historical effort to speak biblically and an attempt to retain the distinction created by that fragmentation. Those congregations not using an instrument of music in worship employ the term **Church of Christ** almost exclusively. Among those using the instrument, both of the Christian Church (Disciples of Christ) and the more conservative "independent" churches, **Christian Church** is most often used. With the "independents" usage varies according to locality. In some areas where others speak of themselves as the **Church of Christ, Christian Church** is used if confusion with others might result.

Beyond question, **Christian Church** and **Church of Christ** were used interchangeably for years without regard to controversies of their time. My family came from a non-instrumental congregation in Western Michigan. The church record at the time of its organization in 1893 describes it as the "Christian Church of Summit," but the deed to the property calls it "The Church of Christ," and it has always been known as the Summit Church of Christ. [9]

As controversial issues began to separate brethren in Christ, each element tended to adopt one of these terms to the exclusion of the other. In 1901 a suit was brought against the church in Hammond, Illinois, to eject it from its house of worship. The suit against the congregation, which did not use an instrument of music in worship, was initiated by a group of dissenters favoring the instrument and calling itself the **Christian Church of Hammond, Illinois.** It was charged that the church, now known as the Church of Christ, had seceded from the Christian Church because the church property was originally registered in the name of the Christian Church. The case reached the Supreme Court of the State of Illinois which on December 18, 1901, ruled in favor of the congregation, stating that "The Church of Christ" had not seceded from the "Christian Church." The court declared:

"Counsel for the appellee say that it is clearly established by the evidence that the original society formed in Hammond was known and recognized by several different names or titles. It was called 'Church of Christ,' 'Disciples of Christ,' and the 'Christian Church,' and these terms were identical in meaning, and used to designate persons of the same religious belief who were members of the same religious denomination." [10]

Three years later a similar case involving the church at Sand Creek, Illinois, also reached the Illinois Supreme Court. As in the Hammond case, it revolved around the terms "Church of Christ" and "Christian Church," and identified each with a specific doctrinal position. The court ruled in favor of the Sand Creek church which occupied similar doctrinal ground to that of the Hammond congregation. [11]

It is evident that the exclusive use of **Church of Christ** and **Christian Church** by distinct elements in the Restoration Movement resulted from a deliberate effort on the part of some to erect a barrier between them. It was a sectarian action in that neither term was applied to the entire undenominational body of the saved, but rather to a group of churches adhering to a specific doctrinal position. The biblical defense of either term was often a rationalization for a denominational act. Those in the Restoration Movement of today have inherited their terminology from another generation. It is time to reexamine our language in light of the scriptures.

The way we talk has a way of letting others see our true colors. Once as Simon Peter warmed himself at the fire while he observed the trial of Jesus from a distance, he denied with an oath that he was a disciple of the Lord. But the truth became evident when one of the bystanders asserted, "The way you talk gives you away" (Matthew 26:73—N.A.S.V.).

Those who are heirs of the Restoration Movement and who seek to be **Christians only** have done the same thing with their terminology. Pick up almost any religious paper and countless church bulletins and observe how frequently the writers use the term **church of Christ** in a sectarian manner. The following is from an article entitled, "The Plight of the Church of Christ Liberal" by one who is currently a Presbyterian pastor. The

90

article is one of two responding to a letter to the editor respecting the one who finds himself out of step with fellow Christians. The quotation is perhaps a bit extreme, but it is nevertheless typical of language frequently heard:

"My childhood was of the strict and straight Church of Christ variety. As a teenager, I was the moral and doctrinal exemplar of Church of Christ orthodoxy. I memorized all the scriptures that are important to the Church of Christ. I mesmerized myself with the Church of Christ doctrines and vigorously defended 'the Lord's church.' I was proud of my religion. I was conscientious and zealous. I chose to go to a Church of Christ college because of my affection for the Church of Christ doctrines." [12]

Notice that in the space of seven sentences the writer uses the phrase **Church of Christ** no less than six times in an unbiblical way. By "Church of Christ doctrine" he does not refer to Bible teaching, but to the pronouncements of a sect. In reading current religious publications one frequently reads of "Church of Christ preachers," "Church of Christ members," and even "Church of Christ churches." Why not say gospel preacher instead of "Church of Christ preacher"? He is proclaiming the good news, not the church. Why not say "Christian" instead of "Church of Christ members" or "members of the Church of Christ"? True, if one is in Christ he is in Christ's body, and therefore a member of His church. But are we willing to affirm that when one speaks of himself as a "Church of Christ member," or more likely, "Church-a-Christ member" as the phrase is slurred together, he is not using the designation in the same sectarian sense as one who calls himself a Baptist or Methodist? Some even go so far as to drop the "member" and refer to individual disciples of Jesus as "Church of Christ."

As already noted, **church of Christ** is not a proper name. It shows possession, that the blood bought body of Jesus belongs to him. If there is any lingering doubt that the phrase is misused, have you heard someone remark, "I'm not a member of the church of God; I'm a member of the church of Christ"? Obviously the speaker is striving for identification which often is difficult. Nevertheless, in the non-sectarian sense the church of God is the church of Christ. Now, it is not wrong to describe the Lord's church as the church of Christ because it does belong to Him. But, have we not become sectarian when we use this term, or any similar term, **exclusively** to the point that we would reject a biblical expression such as the "church of God"? When speaking of the family of God, why not also call it the church of God or the body of Christ or the church of the Lord or the way, all of which are equally as biblical as the church of Christ?

Some respond by suggesting that the error is in spelling church with a capital "C." They conclude that if you say "church of Christ" instead of "Church of Christ" you are designating the undenominational body instead of a sect. But this ignores several things. In the spoken word the capital "C" and the lower case "c" sound alike. In the written word not one person in a hundred would recognize this fine distinction. While the writer may satisfy his own conscience, he scarcely conveys the message of undenominational Christianity in this fashion.

Another response is that we must have some way of identifying ourselves. If we declare ourselves to be the church of God, someone will misunderstand and confuse us with a group by that name having its headquarters in Anderson, Indiana, or Cleveland, Tennessee. So to circumvent the problem we avoid this biblical designation altogether.

If we call ourselves Christians, others may think we are fanatics by appropriating to our exclusive use a term that the religious world generally accepts. So we take the easy way out and declare ourselves to be members of the church of Christ which, to a denominationally attuned mind, is just another denomination. Our language has communicated what we do not believe. The problems of identification and communication are admittedly difficult and will be discussed in other chapters. But let us not shun biblical terminology simply to evade a problem of understanding.

A few years ago I wrote the editor of a widely circulated religious paper. "In the November 4 issue of _____ two statements caught my attention. One, a part of an editorial, states, 'We recently attended a congregation of the Church of Christ which included responsive reading of Scripture in its order of worship.' The other is a phrase in the lead article, ' . . . in church of Christ churches, colleges, and orphans homes.' These statements, which are typical of the terminology used in _____ and other religious periodicals, are denominational to the core and are symptomatic of a denominational concept of the body of Christ. How, biblically speaking, can you have a 'congregation of the Church of Christ' or 'church of Christ churches'? This isn't even good grammar. If those of us who subscribe to the principle of undenominational Christianity, in actuality as well as in theory, expect to convey to others this conception, it is essential that we first grasp the principle ourselves."

The response from the Director of Periodicals, later the editor, is enlightening. "Knowing just how to describe the 'Church of Christ' journalistically is difficult. You are a Church of Christ preacher. You are a member of the Church of Christ. You attend the Church of Christ. I'm almost certain that you have the words 'Church of Christ' on your building somewhere. And probably, if you have taken advantage of the yellow pages listing, you are listed under 'Church of Christ.' The problem is that our actuality doesn't measure up to our theory, to paraphrase your wording. We think it's time to be candid and acknowledge the state of affairs as they are."

The reply of this editor focuses on the difficult problem of identification. That actuality does not always measure up to theory is assuredly true. But in this response there is a certain fatalistic attitude which says in effect, "The plea to be just Christians has not worked. We ought to abandon it and admit our denominational status." It is our conviction that the thesis of undenominational Christianity is still valid, and imperfections of thought, speech, and action which betray denominational tendencies should be squarely faced and corrected rather than accepted.

This is not to suggest that biblical terminology should be avoided because it is misused. The body of Christ is still the church of Christ because He died for it. But care should be taken not to use any term in such an exclusive ways as to attach to it a sectarian concept. If one will use a variety of biblical expressions when speaking of the body of the saved it will improve his own understanding of the church and more adequately convey the simple plea of undenominational Christianity.

We must also be careful not to employ biblical terms in an unbiblical way. "Church of Christ Christians" is an example of scriptural terminology combined in such a way as to convey an erroneous concept. Each of us would do well to appraise his own speech with a critical eye and make such revisions as necessary in the light of the word of God.

Let us also recognize that misuse of biblical language is the symptom, not the problem. True, misuse of speech makes teaching the principles of undenominational Christianity more difficult and in that sense it is part of the problem. But the real difficulty is that those who use designations incorrectly often do not themselves have a clear concept of undenominational Christianity. Correct the understanding and you will go far in correcting the speech. In pointing out our improper speech we are focusing on a sectarian attitude that we may otherwise not be able to appreciate. For as it was said to Peter, "The way you talk gives you away."

## FOOTNOTES

1. Joseph Franklin and J. A. Headington, **The Life and Times of Benjamin Franklin** (St. Louis: John Burns, 1879), pp. 42, 43.

2. Alexander Campbell, "Campbellism," **Christian Baptist,** June 2, 1828.

3. Frank G. Allen, "Christians or Campbellites," **The Old Path Guide,** November, 1879, pp. 431, 432.

4. As late as 1881 **Chambers's Encyclopedia** (Philadelphia: J. B. Lippincott, 1881), refers to those associated with the Restoration Movement as Campbellites. See article, "Religion," vol. 8, p. 179.

5. Franklin and Headington, **Op. cit.,** p. 319.

6. Moses E. Lard, "Abuse of the Name Christian," **Lard's Quarterly,** April, 1865, p. 286.

7. F. G. Allen, **The Old Path Guide,** September, 1879, p. 356.

8. J. H. Garrison, "What Is Our Mission?", **The Christian,** July 8, 1880.

9. Harold E. Hawley, **Lighthouse of Truth, A History of the Summit Church of Christ of Ludington, Michigan** (Milwaukee: Monroe Hawley, 1967), pp. 22-24.

10. W. Carl Ketcherside, "Brothers at Law," **Mission Messenger,** March, 1962, p. 5.

11. **Ibid.,** pp. 6-9.

12. Wayne Willis, "The Plight of the Church of Christ Liberal," **Mission,** June, 1973, pp. 9, 10.

# CHAPTER 8
# THE IMPLICATIONS OF BAPTISM

"Will you be so good as to let me know how any one becomes a Christian? . . . Does the name of Christ or Christian belong to any but those who believe the **gospel,** repent, and are buried by baptism into the death of Christ?" [1]

With these words a Christian lady in Lunenberg, Virginia, questioned Alexander Campbell in a letter dated July 8, 1837. And with these same words she went to the heart of one of the most debated questions in the Restoration Movement. To whom does the word Christian properly apply? How does baptism relate to the right to wear this name?

Undenominational Christianity, especially as it pertains to the Restoration Movement, cannot be discussed without a thorough examination of the place of baptism in one's relationship to God. What one regards as the borders of the kingdom will inevitably be measured in part by the importance he attaches to the biblical concept of baptism.

The development in the Nineteenth Century Reformation of a scriptural understanding of baptism was gradual. It involved the questions of the proper subjects of baptism, its action, and its purpose. Barton W. Stone and the Campbells, coming from Presbyterian background, originally held to infant baptism, sprinkling, and did not relate the ordinance to the remission of sins. In time they renounced all of these positions and accepted as scriptural the immersion of the believer for the remission of sins.

Initially in the Stone movement the action of baptism was not deemed important. Along with the related efforts of Elias Smith and Abner Jones in New England, and James O'Kelly in Virginia, sprinkling was accepted as biblical baptism. Study of God's word, however, convinced Stone that immersion fitted the apostolic pattern. Soon after the dissolution of the Springfield Presbytery Stone and his co-workers assembled to discuss the matter. They concluded that they should be immersed, and since the Baptists would not immerse them, they immersed one another. [2] It was not long before immersion became the accepted practice among them. In 1827 Stone related in his publication what had occurred and gave a picture of the situation as it then stood:

"A number of us from reading the Bible had received the conviction that immersion was the Apostolic mode of baptism, and that believers were the only proper subjects of it. The Elders and brethren met in Conference on this and other subjects of importance. It was unanimously agreed that every brother and sister should act according to their faith; that we should not judge one another for being baptized, or for not being baptized in this mode. The far greater part of the Churches submitted to be baptized by immersion, and now there is not one in 500 among us who has not been immersed." [3]

About the same time Stone concluded from diligent study of God's word that the purpose of baptism is the remission of sins. However, when he quoted Peter's words, "Repent and be baptized . . . for the remission of sins," he found his audience unresponsive and for a number of years did not emphasize this in his teaching. Later he was influenced by Alexander Campbell to revive his convictions. At the time of fusion of the Stone and Campbell forces there was general agreement on the purpose of baptism, although those associated with Stone placed less emphasis on the remission of sins than did Campbell's associates.

To Alexander Campbell must go the credit for clarification of the teaching on baptism in the Restoration Movement. Carl Spain, in an article on "Baptism in the Early Restoration Movement," details the progress of Campbell's thinking in this way:

(1) His interest was kindled by reading the proof sheets of his father's **Declaration and Address** in October, 1809. This prompted an earnest study of the scriptures on the subject.

(2) The birth of his first child, a daughter, in 1812, compelled

him to reach a conclusion on infant baptism and immersion. He became convinced that believer's baptism is taught in the New Testament, and after some discussion with him persuaded Matthias Luse, a Baptist preacher, to immerse him and six others including his wife and parents, on June 12, 1812. Rejecting the usual Baptist confession he was immersed "into the belief that Jesus is the one Christ."

(3) Campbell first suggested the remission of sins as the purpose of baptism in his debate with John Walker, a Presbyterian preacher, in 1820. Although he did not press the point in this debate, Campbell declared:

"Baptism is connected with the promise of the remission of sins, and the gift of the holy spirit." [4]

(4) In 1823 Campbell conducted a debate with W. D. McCalla, another Presbyterian preacher. In it he enlarged on the theme of remission of sins which he had first suggested in the debate three years earlier.

(5) Also in 1823 Campbell began publication of the **Christian Baptist** through which he was destined to wield so much influence on the western frontier. In it there is considerable evidence that his views on baptism were reaching maturity. During this same period he and Walter Scott mutually influenced one another in their thinking on the subject. [5]

It was in 1827 that Walter Scott, having been hired by the Mahoning Baptist Association as its evangelist, first began preaching baptism for the remission of sins. Quoting Acts 2:38 as his proof, he had astounding success and in a matter of months had baptized hundreds. Scott's teaching is a landmark, not because it was the first time this understanding of baptism had been set forth in the Restoration Movement, but because it marked the turning point in public teaching on the subject. Within a few years all within the brotherhood of the Restoration Movement were teaching that baptism is the act of gospel obedience which procures the forgiveness of sins. To Scott also goes the credit for the five finger exercise of salvation—faith, repentance, baptism, remission of sins, gift of the Holy Spirit. This was easy to understand and came to be frequently repeated. It is, of course, an oversimplification of the scheme of redemption as it relates to man's acceptance of the atonement. Faith is not isolated from repentance and baptism. Repentance is faith turning and baptism is faith obeying. There is an interrelationship which is not evident in Scott's five finger exercise. His model of the gospel plan is correct so far as it goes, but study of the scheme of redemption should be pursued beyond it.

Acceptance of the doctrine of immersion for the remission of sins posed some new questions in the Restoration Movement. If one reaches the atoning blood of Christ when he is immersed, what about the condition of the unimmersed? Have their sins been forgiven? Furthermore, is a correct understanding of the purpose of baptism essential at the time one is immersed? And what is the condition of the pious unimmersed who have sought to follow Christ according to their best understanding of God's word? Are they Christians?

This last question was the one raised by the lady from Lunenberg in the letter quoted at the beginning of this chapter. She had noticed Campbell's statement that he could "find in all Protestant parties Christians." How could he, she wondered, reconcile this with his view that baptism is for the remission of sins?

Under the heading, "Any Christians Among Protestant Parties," Campbell issued a lengthy reply. Although he steadfastly held to immersion for the remission of sins, Campbell stated:

" . . . there are Christians among the sects.

"But who is a Christian? I answer, Every one that believes in his heart that Jesus of Nazareth is the Messiah, the Son of God; repents of his sins, and obeys him in all things according to the measure of knowledge of his will. **A perfect man in Christ,** or a perfect Christian, is one thing; and 'a babe in Christ,' a stripling in the faith, or an imperfect Christian, is another. The New Testament recognizes both the perfect man and the imperfect man in Christ . . . .

"I cannot, therefore, make any one duty the standard of Christian state or character, not even immersion into the name of the Father, of the Son, and of the Holy Spirit, and in my heart regard all that have been sprinkled in infancy without their own knowledge and consent, as aliens from Christ and the well-grounded hope of heaven . . . .

"There is no occasion, then, for making immersion, on a profession of the faith, absolutely essential to a Christian— though it may be greatly essential to his sanctification and comfort. My right hand and my right eye are greatly essential to my usefulness and happiness, but not to my life; and as I could not be a perfect man without them, so I cannot be a perfect Christian without a right understanding and a cordial reception of immersion in its true and scriptural meaning and design. But he that thence infers that none are Christians but the immersed, as greatly errs as he who affirms that none are alive but those of clear and full vision." [6]

In this article and two which followed in succeeding issues of the **Millennial Harbinger,** Campbell made it clear that he was not referring to those who, understanding the scripture, refuse to obey it. Nor was he advocating the acceptance of the unimmersed into membership of the local church.

Campbell's response to the Lunenberg letter set off a storm of protest by those who felt he had abandoned his position and given comfort to the sectarians. In his defense he pointed out that on numerous occasions he had referred to Christians among the sects without anyone's taking exception. His views, he concluded, had not changed. His purpose in replying as explicitly as he did to the lady from Lunenberg was to counteract some "ultras" in Eastern Virginia who had gone to extremes. [7]

It is likely that most agreed with Campbell's conclusion that there are Christians among the sects, but probably many had not realized that among these he was including some unimmersed. Many of them had earlier been Baptists and they regarded themselves as Christians when a part of that denomination. But now that Campbell made it clear that he included those who had been sprinkled as among the Christians he found within the sects, there was strong disapproval.

The question of whether the "pious unimmersed" are Christians was to arise frequently in the Restoration Movement. In 1861 and 1862 there was a controversy in the religious papers on "Communion with the Sects." It related to whether the unimmersed should be invited to partake of the Lord's supper. More fundamental than the question itself, however, was the one which was behind the reasoning of the disputants—are the unimmersed Christians? W. K. Pendleton, son-in-law of Campbell, reaffirmed Campbell's view expressed twenty-five years earlier:

"We all agreed that he who willfully or negligently perverts the outward, cannot have the inward. But can he who, through a simple mistake, involving no perversity of mind, has misapprehended the outward baptism, yet submitting to it according to his view of it, have the inward baptism, which changes his state, and has the praise of God, though not of all men? is the precise question. To which I answer, that in my opinion, it is possible." [8]

Isaac Errett, longtime editor of the **Christian Standard** and one of the most influential men in the Restoration Movement, felt that to deny that the unimmersed are Christians would be to damage the plea for Christian unity. He wrote:

"We trust Bro. F (ranklin) will allow us to counsel him not to damage this great plea for Christian union by a spirit of exclusiveness which will only allow of 'supposed piety and Christianity' in neighboring denominations, which refuses to recognize as Christians all the unimmersed, and claims for ourselves to be Christians par excellence, because of a bit of accuracy on the question of baptism." [9]

Two points are evident in these comments. Pendleton thought the condition of the heart might confer the approval of God upon those unimmersed who did not fully understand the import of the ordinance. Errett seemed to devalue immersion's importance in speaking of "a bit of accuracy on the question of baptism." The question may be put this way: is a mistake in the observance of baptism, which puts one into the family of God, no more vital than a misunderstanding of some doctrines once one is in Christ?

The other side was stated by Benjamin Franklin, editor of the **American Christian Review,** and probably the most influential man in the movement at that time:

"Can these brethren show that the Lord receives or pardons persons without baptism, or before they are baptized? If they can, then they are Christians, disciples of Christ, and in the kingdom, and not only have a right to commune, but an equal right to enjoy any other privilege in the kingdom, or even to be received into the church itself. If it can not be shown that persons are in the kingdom, in Christ, received of the Lord, and pardoned before baptism, or without baptism, then it cannot be proved that they are Christians before, or without baptism, and persons who cannot be shown to be Christians, certainly cannot be shown to be communicants." [10]

Franklin wanted to settle the question by the teaching of Scripture. He was willing to accept the unbaptized as fellow Christians only if it could be demonstrated from the Bible that they had been pardoned by God. Others felt that this was a legalistic approach and believed that our feelings about others based on our observation constitute a valid way of determining their relationship to God. This is essentially an emotional appeal, well summed up recently by Logan Fox:

"Our biggest problem, I think, is our stand on immersion. Our hearts and minds tell us that people baptized by sprinkling are Christians, as witness our use of their hymns in our worship, our use of their reference materials in our study of the Bible, and our use of their sermon books in the preparation of our sermons. But our doctrinal logic tells us that they **cannot** be Christians because they have not been immersed." [11]

The fallacy of this approach is that it determines relationships on the basis of feeling rather than by the authority of the word of God. Reasoning the same way, Peter and his companions could have said, "Our hearts tell us that Cornelius is a Christian. He is devout, he is God fearing, he is a liberal giver, and he constantly prays. In these respects he exceeds the righteousness of most people we count as God's children. Therefore he must be in a saved condition." But Luke informs us that in spite of his many "Christian" characteristics, Cornelius was lost (Acts 11:14). We should remember that it is the Lord, not we, who determines who are the saved. We must rely upon what he has told us about those whom he accepts rather than to let our feelings govern our conclusions.

At the risk of being charged with legalism, let us make a few observations:

(1) The New Testament teaches that baptism is immersion (Romans 6:3, 4; Colossians 2:12).
(2) The New Testament teaches that immersion is for the remission of sins (Acts 2:38; 22:16).
(3) No one in apostolic times was considered to be a Christian or to have had his sins forgiven without immersion.

Few associated with any element of the Restoration Movement, past or present, would be disposed to disagree with these conclusions. Now, proceeding on the assumption that these statements are true, we simply are not on firm biblical ground to assume that one is forgiven, and hence a Christian, without having been immersed.

In a discussion some years ago a brother in Christ argued that it is the act of commitment that makes one a Christian, although baptism should express one's outward commitment to Christ. On this basis he reasoned that one, who, not understanding the full import of baptism, is sprinkled has by this act had his sins remitted. I inquired what he would do should the man later recognize that immersion is biblical baptism. He replied that he would immerse him. "Why?" I inquired. "According to your logic his sins have already been forgiven." To which he retorted with a smile, "I guess I'm still that much of a legalist." But the point is still valid. If one who is honestly mistaken gets right with God without immersion, we cannot ask him to be immersed for the remission of sins since he has already received pardon. And if we do not immerse him, on what basis can we ask others to be immersed for forgiveness since we have in effect rejected the doctrine?

If we accept the teaching that immersion procures the remission of sins, we have no right to contend that those who have not complied with this ordinance have received God's blessing of forgiveness. God has not granted us the right to extend that blessing to others, however much we may admire their characters as representative of what Jesus would have us be.

Does this mean that there is no possibility of the unimmersed going to heaven? It does not. We are not the judges. Through study of the word of God we learn of those to whom salvation is promised. It is our responsibility to teach what we find in the New Testament. We dare not go beyond this nor promise anything which the Bible does not. On the other hand, neither is it our place to pronounce eternal judgment on any soul. The same one who told his apostles, "He who believes and is baptized will be saved," will also be the judge at the last day. His judgment will be according to mercy and justice. He will do what is right, whatever that may be. If he chooses to set aside the requirement of immersion and extend clemency to the unimmersed, we have no right to tell him that he has done wrong. Since he has given the command, he also has the right to rescind it if he desires. A judge may take into account extenuating circumstances if he chooses. But the law, if we think of the dispensation of grace in a legal sense for a moment, remains. Acquittal is obtained on the basis of clemency, not by an arbitrary change of the law.

This is not to say that Christ will or will not act in this fashion on the day of judgment. He has not said what he will do. Each one has the right of personal opinion on the matter, but no one has the right to commit the Lord to a course of action. Whether he will save the ignorant person who has never heard of Christ is up to him. But since he has not promised to redeem him, we must act upon the assumption that the gospel of Christ is the only means of his salvation and do our best to take him that message.

In the meantime, let's retire from the judging business and let the Lord decide whom he will save. Our responsibility is to teach God's redeeming grace appropriated by the penitent believer through immersion, and to leave the destiny of those who do not so respond in the hands of God.

If our reasoning is sound, it follows that the undenominational body of Christ is circumscribed by the ordinance of immersion. It is apparent that one of the twin objectives proposed by the early reformers must be reevaluated in terms of this limitation. When the ideal of Christian union on the platform of the authority of the scriptures was proposed by Stone and the Campbells, these men did not envision the impact that their later insistence on immersion would have on their plea. Initially they drew people from the pedobaptists as well as the immersionists. This was especially true of those associated with Stone. But as they began to insist on immersion, those observing sprinkling were not so willing to unite with them because it meant the surrender of a cherished practice. The merging of the Stone and Campbell forces was regarded as practical evidence of the validity of the plea for Christian union. Since both groups practiced immersion, baptism **was not a major problem. It is a fact, however, that most** major religious groups are not immersionists. If one insists that immersion is a prerequisite to admittance to the family of God, how can he call for Christian union with those who have not yet acknowledged this truth by their personal actions?

The liberal element in the movement sought to resolve this problem by removing baptism from its position of importance in the kingdom of God. While outwardly continuing to stand for immersion as the best expression of one's acceptance of Jesus, they played down the function of immersion that procures forgiveness through the blood of Christ. Thus in effect they were saying, "We differ on baptism, but this isn't really more important than other matters of disagreement. Let's work as fellow Christians for unity." Their continued stress on Christian union was at the expense of a fundamental teaching of God's word.

Once a changed attitude toward baptism was assumed it was inevitable that some would want to practice open-membership, the acceptance of the unimmersed into fellowship. As early as 1885 W. T. Moore began advocating that those who had been sprinkled should be accepted if they sincerely believed they were right. In 1892 or 1893 the Lennox Avenue Church in New York City introduced a modified form of open membership. It invited the unimmersed to be accepted as members of the congregation or Christians on the basis of their previous baptism, but not as Disciples of Christ. This was clearly a sectarian position since it made a distinction between a Christian and a Disciple of Christ. The Cedar Avenue Church in Cleveland introduced a form of open membership in 1894, and the Monroe Street Church in Chicago did so in 1906. By 1929 only nineteen churches among the Disciples were "openly and avowedly" committed to the practice, but A. T. DeGroot observed that many ministers were practicing it, with or without church approval. [12] Since that time a large percentage of the liberal Disciple churches have adopted the practice.

Open membership was a long time in coming because it meant the surrender of a basic position. If the undenominational body is indeed limited to those who have been biblically baptized, there is no way that open membership can be justified. It would perhaps be correct to state that those churches that have adopted the practice had already rejected undenominational Christianity and the restoration plea as historically understood.

Two other questions relating to baptism should be considered in relation to our subject. Does the validity of one's baptism hinge upon the baptizer? Some have contended that unless one is baptized by a "Church of Christ preacher" he is not scripturally baptized. It would be difficult to find a more sectarian teaching than this. A moment's reflection should show that whether one is accepted by God does not depend upon the administrator, but on the subject himself. How could one positively determine that the one baptizing him is right with God? If the validity of one's baptism depends upon the baptizer, then it follows that the validity of the baptizer's baptism, in turn, depends upon who baptized him. You have a chain not unlike the Catholic doctrine of apostolic succession in which one is not considered properly ordained unless all of those in the chain of ordination back to the apostles were also properly ordained. Break the chain in but one place and all succeeding ordinations are nullified. None of us can trace a baptismal chain of baptizers even two hundred years, let alone nearly two thousand. Even Alexander Campbell was baptized by a Baptist preacher. The matter has been well summed up by G. C. Brewer:

"The whole point, then, turns upon the individual's attitude— his motive, his faith, his repentance, his obedience. It is not a question of whether what the denomination teaches is true or untrue; it is a question of what the individual did, and no one can say what he did but the individual himself. He must determine the matter in the light of what he now knows God's word to teach and with a clear memory of what he did." [13]

"But," someone objects, "you cannot be taught wrong and be baptized right." There is in this an unstated assumption, not necessarily true, that the understanding of the one being baptized is the same as that of the one baptizing him. Convictions can result from a combination of influences. One might, for instance, learn from a radio sermon that baptism is immersion and from a friend at work that it is for the remission of sins. It is totally unfair to say to any individual, "You were not scripturally baptized because the one who baptized you did not have a correct understanding." Each case must be considered on its own merits. Let us teach the truth of God's word, make sure that the individual understands it, and then let him be the judge of whether he has complied with what we mutually agree is taught in Scripture. To require a person to be baptized again to please the church when he vows that he understood what he was doing the first time is mockery since it would be to please the church, not his Lord.

Neither are we justified in seeking to invalidate another's baptism because the baptizer, although correct in his teaching relating to salvation, practices doctrinal error in other areas. That he may err regarding the Lord's supper, music in the worship, or church organization is totally unrelated to those he immerses into Jesus. True, he may lead them astray after their acceptance of Christ, but if they have obeyed from the heart the good news of Jesus, they do not need to be reborn into the family of God on that account.

Finally, some attention should be given to another matter that has periodically been discussed in the Restoration Movement. This relates to the degree of understanding of the purpose of baptism required at the time of one's obedience to the gospel. In 1832 John Thomas, an English physician, immigrated to the United States. For several years he was a gospel preacher, doing most of his work in Eastern Virginia. About 1835 he began to advocate through a paper he published that unless one is baptized with the specific understanding that the purpose of baptism is for the remission of sins, his baptism is invalid. Among other things he concluded that immersion by denominationalists such as Presbyterians, Episcopalians, or Catholics was invalid because the administrator preached a different gospel than that revealed in the scriptures. [14] His major contention, however, related to Baptist immersion which he asserted was unacceptable to God because it was not for the remission of sins.

Thomas' teaching prompted a letter to Alexander Campbell by a Christian lady writing under the name of "Sharon." She and others were sorely troubled by whether they should be reimmersed since their prior immersion had been at the hands of Baptists. Campbell published her letter and took strong exception to the position of Thomas. Seeing a parallel to the circumcision controversy in Acts 15 in which the Gentiles were not required to be circumcised, Campbell wrote:

"And am I asked, **Who is a citizen of the kingdom of heaven?** I answer, every one who believes in his heart that Jesus of Nazareth is the Messiah the Son of God, and publicly confesses his faith in his death for our sins, in his burial and resurrection, by an immersion into the name of the Father, the Son, and the Holy Spirit. Every such person is a constitutional citizen of Christ's kingdom . . . .

"If every one that does not clearly understand the meaning of baptism at the time of his immersion, or afterwards, is, on that account, an alien and 'in his sins;' then were the Apostles very remiss in not preaching re-immersion to the church of God in Rome; for Paul had to explain to them the meaning of baptism, chapter VI . . . . " [15]

Campbell conceded that it may be questionable whether those expressly immersed **because** their sins previously had been forgiven ought to be regarded as ignorant and, therefore should be reimmersed. [16] However, he concluded that most Baptists did not fall into this category and were simply wanting in a full understanding of the purpose of baptism.

The controversy between Thomas and Campbell continued for several years, gradually embracing other issues relating to Thomas' speculations regarding the future. Campbell finally denounced him in the **Millennial Harbinger.** In 1844 Thomas announced that existing churches in the Restoration Movement were apostate and began the group that later became known as the Christadelphians. [17]

It should be noted that neither Stone nor the Campbells nor most of the early preachers in the Restoration Movement understood when they were baptized the relationship between baptism and the remission of sins. These men were not baptized again when they reached a fuller understanding. This has nothing to do with the truth or falsity of Thomas' position, but it is a fact that needs to be remembered.

In 1884 Austin McGary of Texas began publishing the **Firm Foundation**. His purpose was to combat the practice of some preachers of "shaking in the Baptists," the accepting into fellowship of those who were immersed, not for the remission of sins, but because their sins had already been forgiven. McGary felt they should be reimmersed. David Lipscomb took exception in the **Gospel Advocate** to McGary's position. A lengthy discussion between them took place in 1890 in the periodicals edited by the two men. For fifteen years the matter was widely controverted. J. N. Armstrong once stated that feelings ran so high that when one crossed the Mississippi River he was immediately suspect as he left the territory of the **Advocate** or **Foundation** and passed into the area of influence of the other. Eventually the issue abated with a general agreement that each case should be decided individually.

Lipscomb felt that if a person were baptized for the motive of wanting to obey God, this purpose was acceptable, even if he did not fully comprehend that baptism is for the remission of sins. McGary insisted that God requires an accurate understanding of the purpose of baptism. Lipscomb, himself, when asked by Tolbert Fanning at the age of fourteen why he wanted to be baptized, replied, "To obey God." [18]

Two things should be evident in this discussion. One is that immersion for a totally wrong purpose is unacceptable to God. Should one be baptized to please a mate, to improve business relations, to go along with the crowd, or to join a human denomination, he could hardly expect the Lord to accept his obedience as meeting the divine requirements. On the other hand, very few people at the time of their baptism completely understand the significance of the ordinance. Not everyone who recognizes that baptism is for the remission of sins realizes that it is also a likeness of the death, burial, and resurrection of Christ (Romans 6:1-6). To be identified with Christ in his death is just as truly a purpose of baptism as is the remission of sins. Entire sermons have often been preached on "What Must I Do to be Saved?" without once mentioning the blood of Christ. Is it not possible that some have been immersed as a result of such teaching with the conviction that baptism is for the remission of sins, but without realizing that the atonement has anything to do with it?

All teachers of the word should seek to paint the whole picture of salvation to the truth seeker. This is the surest way to remove any doubt that the obedient believer understands what he is doing. But let us also acknowledge that there is a difference in being baptized for the wrong purpose and in not completely understanding every aspect of the purpose of baptism. One's understanding may be less than perfect and still please God, but it can hardly be totally in error and still be acceptable to him. What degree of understanding Christ may require we do not propose to answer, but certainly each situation should be measured by its own merits in relation to the divine teaching.

## FOOTNOTES

1. Correspondent, "Any Christians Among Protestant Parties," **Millennial Harbinger,** September, 1837, p. 411.

2. John Rogers, **The Biography of Elder Barton Warren Stone** (Cincinnati: J. A. and U. P. James, 1847), pp. 60, 61.

3. B. W. Stone, **The Christian Messenger,** October 25, 1827.

4. Alexander Campbell, **Debate on Christian Baptism between John Walker and Alexander Campbell** (Pittsburgh: Eichbaum and Johnston, 1822), p. 13.

5. Carl Spain, "Baptism in the Early Restoration Movement," **Restoration Quarterly,** vol. 1, no. 4, 1957, pp. 215-217.

6. Alexander Campbell, "Any Christians Among Protestant Parties," **Millennial Harbinger,** September, 1837, pp. 411, 412, 414.

7. The "ultras" to whom Campbell referred were those influenced by Dr. John Thomas in Eastern Virginia. Dr. Thomas lived about twenty-five miles from Lunenberg. A year after Campbell received the letter from Lunenberg he held a public discussion with Thomas at Amelia, Virginia, which was attended by a number of Christians from Lunenberg. Although baptism apparently was not one of the subjects discussed at that time, the two men did have differences in this area which later contributed to Thomas' leaving the movement.

8. W. K. Pendleton, **Millennial Harbinger,** April, 1862, p. 181.

9. Isaac Errett, **Millennial Harbinger,** March, 1862, p. 131.

10. Benjamin Franklin, "The Communion Question," **Millennial Harbinger,** July, 1862, p. 299.

11. Logan Fox, "Destiny or Disease?", **Voices of Concern** (St. Louis: Mission Messenger, 1966), pp. 29, 30.

12. Alfred T. DeGroot, **The Grounds of Divisions Among the Disciples of Christ** (Chicago: privately published, 1940), p. 189.

13. G. C. Brewer, **Contending for the Faith** (Nashville: Gospel Advocate, 1941), p. 167.

14. John Thomas, "Re-Immersion and Brother Thomas," **Millennial Harbinger,** February, 1836, p. 60.

15. Alexander Campbell, "Re-Immersion," **Millennial Harbinger,** September, 1835, p. 419.

16. Alexander Campbell, "Re-Immersion and Brother Thomas, **Millennial Harbinger,** November, 1835, p. 565-567.

17. The issue of baptism does not seem to have been so important in the departure of Thomas as his multitude of speculations relating to the state of the dead and eternal punishment and reward.

18. Earl I. West, **The Search for the Ancient Order** (Indianapolis: Religious Book Service, 1950), vol. 2, pp. 405-407.

# CHAPTER 9
# FREE CHURCHES IN CHRIST

In the fall of 1855 a convention of delegates from five Kentucky congregations of the Restoration Movement founded The Central Kentucky Christian Union.

"The membership was to include all the preachers in those counties, one 'elder' from each church, and one representative for each one hundred members of the churches. The 'Union' was to receive information concerning the condition of the churches, hear any case which might be laid before it, discipline any who should 'teach things tending to the injury of the churches and the cause which we plead.' It was to 'take into consideration the subject of education, both general and ministerial,' and 'consider and act upon plans for Bible distribution, missionary objects, tract distribution, Sunday-schools, and upon whatever else may tend to the welfare of the church of our Divine Master.' It was also to 'co-operate with any other association of our brotherhood, whether district or State meeting, or general convention,' to which it 'may appoint delegates.'" [1]

Clearly the Central Union was a denominational organization. Not only did it presume to make executive decisions for the churches which comprised it, but it also claimed authority over those congregations in judicial affairs. It spoke of "our brotherhood" in the same sense that others might refer to "our denomination." Could a group of churches establish such a structure and still make a valid claim to being undenominational?

One criterion of denominationalism previously suggested in

111

this study is that a religious group is denominational if it has an organization foreign to the word of God. The apostolic church was without any kind of inter-congregational organization. From its beginning the Restoration Movement strongly opposed any structure which even suggested ecclesiasticism. In time, however, the subject of organization was to provoke more discussion and controversy than any other single topic in the history of the effort. In our examination of undenominational Christianity it is pertinent to inquire at what point an association of Christians or of congregations constitutes itself as a sectarian organization.

In the Restoration Movement the tone of opposition to extra-congregational organization was established early. The **Last Will and Testament of the Springfield Presbytery** of 1804 not only called for the abandonment of all denominational organizations, but also set forth the reasons for such a stance. In the "Witnesses' Address" the signers of this amazing document declared how they reached their decision to dissolve their presbytery:

"Their reasons for dissolving that body were the following: With deep concern they viewed the divisions, and party spirit among professing Christians, principally owing to the adoption of human creeds and forms of government. While they were united under the name of a Presbytery, they endeavored to cultivate a spirit of love and unity with all Christians; but found it extremely difficult to suppress the idea that they themselves were a party separate from others . . . . At their last meeting they undertook to prepare for the press a piece entitled Observations on Church Government, in which the world will see the beautiful simplicity of Christian church government, stript of human inventions and lordly traditions. As they proceeded in the investigation of the subject, they soon found that there was neither precept nor example in the New Testament for such confederacies as modern Church Sessions, Presbyteries, Synods, General Assemblies, etc. Hence they concluded, that while they continued in the connection in which they then stood, they were off the foundation of the Apostles and Prophets, of which Christ himself is the chief corner stone. However just, therefore, their view of church government might have been, they would have gone out under the name and sanction of a self-constituted body. Therefore, from a principle of love to Christians of every name, the precious cause of Jesus, and dying sinners who are kept from the Lord by the existence of sects and parties in the church, they have cheerfully consented to retire from the din and fury of conflicting parties—sink out of the view of fleshly minds, and die the death." [2]

In view of this uncompromising stand against human organizations, it is surprising to learn that the congregations associated with the Stone element of the Restoration Movement began a conference system in 1810 with associations being established in Kentucky, Ohio, and Tennessee.[3] These conferences, however, were quite different from the denominational organizations usually implied by the term. Stone commented:

"We as a conference meddle not in the government of the churches, leaving each church to act according to the New Testament. We have no other bonds of union than the bonds of charity, and peace and righteousness, founded on the word of God."[4]

He further described one assembly in this way:

"No bishop was called to the chair, nor was any clergyman or lay-member chosen president. We entered no resolution upon our minute book, nor did we take the name of an 'advisory council.' But with one accord in one place we mutually engaged in arranging the appointments for our next annual meetings so as to promote the cause of the Redeemer."[5]

It is apparent that these conferences were little more than mass meetings comparable to later state meetings and to some current lectureships. They were sessions to edify and encourage, but they acted neither in a legislative, executive, nor judicial capacity. Lacking these elements, did the conferences constitute a denominational structure? We will return to this question shortly.

While the Stone congregations were assembling in their conferences, another development was transpiring among those churches associated with the Campbells. The Campbells had cast their lot early with the Baptists. After withdrawing from the Redstone Baptist Association with which they had been affiliated, the Campbells established a congregation at Wellsburg, Virginia, which in 1824 was accepted into the Mahoning Baptist Association located in the Western Reserve of Ohio. This organization was less ecclesiastical than similar bodies as its constitution indicates:

"It is our object to glorify God. This we would endeavor to do by urging the importance of the doctrine and precepts of the gospel in their moral and evangelical nature, commending ourselves to every man's conscience in the sight of God; not pretending to have authority over any man's(conscience,) nor over the churches, whose representatives form this association. But we act as an advisory counsel only, disclaiming all superiority, jurisdiction, coercive right and infallibility; and acknowledging the independence of every church; which has received authority from Christ to perform all duties enjoined respecting the government of his church in this world." [6]

While claiming to be only an "advisory council" and rejecting the right to intrude on the autonomy of the local congregation, the association nevertheless adopted a creed of thirteen articles. Such an official statement of belief is one of the sure marks of sectarianism, and while it may be argued that the Mahoning Association lacked most of the oppressive characteristics of similar organizations of the day, it was nevertheless a denominational structure in an elemental form.

At the annual meeting of the association in 1827, Walter Scott was appointed to travel as an evangelist in the Western Reserve with the endorsement and financial support of the churches of the association. In this action the Mahoning Association added a new dimension to the "advisory council" concept. Hayden comments:

"In this it took upon itself the new duty of **establishing** and **regulating an evangelical agency, or ministry.**" [7]

It had, in fact, become a missionary society of sorts. It had now assumed an executive capacity for the churches in one of their functions, that of evangelism.

The Campbell influence in the association caused its members to reexamine many of their views in the light of the word of God. Increasingly they called for a "thus saith the Lord" for every teaching and practice. Alexander Campbell himself attacked in **The Christian Baptist** "missionary societies, Bible societies, education societies" which would "rob the church of its glory, and exalt the inventions of men above the wisdom of God." It is not surprising, therefore, that some began to question the legitimacy of the Mahoning Association itself. At its annual meeting in Austintown, Ohio, in 1830, John Henry exhorted the gathering: "I charge you to look out what you are about to do here; we want nothing here which the word of the Lord will not sanction." He quickly moved that the association as an advisory council be dissolved. Immediately the resolution was passed unanimously in spite of personal reservation by Alexander Campbell of the wisdom of the step. The assembly then agreed to gather annually as a mass meeting for mutual edification and for the hearing of reports of the progress of the cause of Christ.

In the meantime, a similar pattern was developing among the Reforming Baptists in Kentucky. The Campbell influence divided many of the associations. Soon after their division, those parts of the Boones' Creek, North District, Bracken, and Licking associations sympathetic to the cause of the Reformers voluntarily dissolved themselves as Baptist organizations.

Following the consolidation of the Stone and Campbell forces in the early 1830's, the Restoration Movement had no organization that any might consider denominational. Christians in distinct geographic areas gathered in "yearly meetings" for fellowship and edification. These meetings assumed no authority and made no decisions. They were simply mass meetings of disciples of Christ. In time they were often replaced by "state meetings" of much the same nature, but on a larger scale.

However, in the 1830's and 1840's congregational cooperation was widely discussed. The yearly meetings soon became "cooperation meetings" with presidents, secretaries, and treasurers. While disavowing any attempt to legislate for the churches, the cooperations set up ways of evangelizing given areas, and chose evangelists who were authorized to preach in their regions with support guaranteed by the cooperations. T. M. Henley proposed that if a congregation was unable by itself to sustain an evangelist it might invite sister churches to cooperate with it and work through it rather than establish an organization outside the local church for the purpose of cooperation. This procedure, he felt, would avoid the ecclesiastical domination that he and others feared would be forthcoming from the cooperations. [8]

The Cooperation Meetings proved to be forerunners of more structured associations. In 1845 the American Christian Bible Society was established in Cincinnati under the direction of D. S. Burnett. It was followed in 1849 by the American Christian Missionary Society which elected Alexander Campbell as its first president. Its object was "to promote the spread of the gospel in destitute places of our own and foreign lands." Its constitution provided for a president, twenty vice-presidents, a treasurer, and two secretaries. It was to be composed of annual delegates, Life Members, and Life Directors, and membership was contingent upon a membership fee. Although the convention that gave birth to the society was originally conceived as an assembly of delegates from churches, it was attended by many preachers and leaders who had come without specific invitation. Accordingly, everyone in attendance was enrolled as a delegate and to all intents and purposes the assembly was a mass meeting. The American Christian Missionary Society was thus established as an association of individuals rather than of official church delegates.

Concurrently state societies were established in many states to evangelize their areas. As might be expected, there was strong opposition to the societies and to the national society in particular. Earl West summarizes the objections in this way:

"It will be noticed that these objections fell into three classifications. The first of these was based upon the Society's method of membership, viz., making membership depend upon the payment of stipulated amounts of money. The second of these stemmed from the potential danger the Society maintained of infringing upon the independence of a local congregation. The third objection came from the conviction that human organizations were unauthorized in the scriptures, and therefore, were unscriptural."[9]

The society became the first serious wedge dividing those who saw themselves as **Christians only**. It faced growing opposition and serious problems. Its difficulties were compounded during the Civil War when it offended those who supported the Confederacy and others who were pacifists by adopting in 1863, nearly unanimously, a series of pro-Union resolutions. Many thought this constituted an attempt to legislate for the people of God and was a departure into the political arena from the function for which the society was organized.

Accordingly, a compromise called the "Louisville Plan" was effected in 1869 in an effort to placate opponents. The new organization was called the "General Christian Missionary Convention" and its supporters sought to eliminate some of the objections to the society such as the money basis for membership. Its machinery was cumbersome and satisfied neither proponents nor opponents. The General Convention was made up of messengers from state conventions. The state conventions were made up of messengers from churches and district conventions, the latter being composed of local church delegates. In effect the Louisville Plan created the structure of a full-fledged denominational organization. It is not surprising that society enemies did not buy the compromise, for while it could be argued that the American Christian Missionary Society was merely as association of individuals, the new General Convention presumed to speak for the congregations themselves.

Discontentment with the organization led to the establishment in 1875 of the Foreign Christian Missionary society by those who decided that it was useless to try to compromise with implacable opponents. The Louisville Plan was eventually abandoned and organized missionary work through societies reached its low ebb. In 1879 Joseph Franklin wrote:

"The death of the Missionary Society left the churches of the Reformation in precisely the condition as to organization, in which they found themselves after the dissolution of Mahoning Association. There was no longer any representative assembly among them, and every congregation was as free as if it had been the only congregation in existence. The Disciples again settled down upon the principle of pure congregationalism." [10]

The missionary society was not so dead as Franklin thought. A new constitution was adopted in 1881. In 1920 the various societies then existing among the Disciples of Christ were consolidated into the United Christian Missionary Society. A major battle followed in the 1920's, continuing for several decades, between those who saw a menacing ecclesiasticism in the United Society and others who favored an even more structured inter-church government. Many of those concerned about loss of congregational autonomy to the International Convention and the United Society, as well as growing theological liberalism, withdrew in 1927 to begin the rival North American Christian Convention. This convention is essentially a mass meeting similar to college lectureships conducted among Christians who totally reject the society organization.

In September, 1968, the International Convention of Christian Churches (Disciples of Christ) changed its structure from a loose federation of independent congregations to that of an official denominational body with legal affiliation with member churches. State societies are now called regional organizations, and the chief officer of what is now an admitted denomination is its Moderator.

Although the more conservative congregations in the Restoration Movement rejected the missionary society as unbiblical, considerable discussion has continued among them as to the proper means of congregational cooperation. A majority have subscribed to the view that churches may individually contribute of their funds to another congregation for cooperative purposes with that congregation assuming direction of the work being undertaken. Others have rejected this approach as unbiblical. Two prevailing schools of thought have continued since the 1950's with congregations tending to line up on one side or the other.

117

Historical objections to extra-congregational organizations in the Restoration Movement generally fall under two headings. First, they were opposed as being unscriptural, human organizations doing the work of the church without divine warrant. Second, many opposed them on grounds of expediency. Some feared they would lead to ecclesiasticism while others questioned whether they would actually accomplish the purpose for which they were intended. For a consideration of the biblical legitimacy of societies the reader is directed to the voluminous writings on various sides of the issue. The matter of expediency is essentially one of judgment, but it should be observed that something cannot be an expedient if it is disapproved by scripture. On the other hand, something may be scriptural and still be inexpedient. Certainly Paul made this distinction regarding the eating of meats (Romans 14:13-21).

Our concern in this study is whether extra-congregational organizations, such as the missionary societies, are themselves denominational. This question has not been raised so often as whether such bodies are biblical. Many probably see the two issues as the same: if an organization is denominational it follows that it must be unbiblical. However, it is possible for a body to sustain an unbiblical relationship to a congregation without its being a denominational expression of that church. For example, the Red Cross exists outside the church and in the field of benevolence its work may overlap that of the church. The propriety of the church's doing benevolence through the Red Cross would be highly questionable. Many believe it unbiblical. Yet, should a congregation channel all of its benevolent funds through the Red Cross this would not make that organization a religious denomination. Such action would be voluntary with no coercion on part of the Red Cross and no effort to extend its authority over the local church. It makes no attempt to determine the policies of a congregation.

Apostolic congregations, so far as the New Testament picture is concerned, were entirely independent in the operation of their affairs. True, the apostles exercised authority in the doctrinal realm, but their function was temporary and with their death we can find no hierarchy, no organization larger than the local church deciding its policies. Extra-congregational organizations through which the Lord's work was done did exist, but they were not part of the organizational structure of the church. Paul utilized the school of Tyranus (Acts 19:9) to proclaim the word of God, but nothing in the text implies that it became a denominational outreach of the church. So far as we can learn each congregation was autonomous. Autonomy is "self-law" or "self-government." When this right is surrendered by congregations to another organization, the body assuming that right and the churches over which it exercises some measure of control have constituted a denominational association.

Present day congregations work through a variety of organizations to further the cause of Christ. Newspapers publish ads to promote the church, time is purchased from broadcasting stations to proclaim the good news, and even the postal service distributes weekly bulletins of congregations. Religious papers, Christian colleges, and children's homes are established by Christians to perform services in their respective areas. At what point, we must ask, do any of these become part of a denominational structure? Certainly they do not by reason of the church's spending money with them, even should such expenditure be unwise or unbiblical. If a congregation chooses to hire the services of an extra-congregational organization, or even contribute money to it, it has merely exercised its right of self-government. However, when an organization receiving funds from congregations presumes to determine the policies of the churches or make their decisions or settle their disputes, that body and the congregations related to it have set up a denominational structure. The Central Kentucky Christian Union was not sectarian because churches contributed to it, but because it usurped the authority of congregations in their affairs.

We earlier inquired whether the conferences of the Stone movement were denominational. If Barton Stone correctly described them, and we believe he did, they could hardly be considered such since they exercised no authority. That they were called conferences does not alter the picture. Most religious conferences are ecclesiastical. The Stone conferences were for the purpose of "conferring." It is the function of an assembly that determines its role, not the title employed.

And what of the missionary societies that have existed within the Restoration Movement? Have they, and do they, erode the automomy of the local church? Should a society serve only to receive and spend voluntary contributions, a legitimate charge of usurping authority would be hard to establish. The original constitution of the American Christian Missionary Society does not reveal an organization usurping local church autonomy. As with many colleges, publishing houses, and youth camps today, it was composed of individuals. It did not purport to tell churches what to do with their funds. Although biblically challenged on the ground that it was doing missionary work which should be carried on by churches, it was not initially a denominational body

119

intruding on the affairs of local congregations.

Practically speaking, however, the society soon overstepped its stated objectives. It obtained from Alexander Campbell publishing rights to the Christian Hymn Book. The Hymn Book Committee then issued the following announcement:

"This Hymn Book is the result of an agreement between Alexander Campbell—the former proprietor of the Christian Hymn Book—and the Christian brotherhood at large, as represented in the American Christian Missionary Society." [11]

Whether it had been so intended to act or not, the society was now viewed by some such as the Hymn Book Committee as a denominational organ. This became more evident during the Civil War when the pro-Union political pronouncements were made. A major motivation for the action was to declare to the world the loyalty of the "Disciples brotherhood." The resolutions were clearly denominational declarations of a denominational body.

Although Moses E. Lard was a defender of the missionary society's right to exist, like many of his time he was concerned that such an organization would usurp the autonomy of churches and become an ecclesiastical body. He wrote:

"Missionary Societies are dangerous institutions. Not in themselves, of course, or when doing right, or acting within their own proper bounds; but dangerous because of their extreme liability to usurp power which does not belong to them, and to perform acts hurtful and oppressive to the feelings of God's children, which they can not lawfully perform. No man living can say that the danger here does not exist, or that it is imaginary. The tendency of all human instititutions, especially of all moneyed and chartered institutions, is to augment continually their power, that thereby they may become the more effective in their operations . . . . But their most dangerous features lie, not in their efforts to preserve themselves, but in their usurpation and use of unwarrantable power." [12]

Lard buttressed his position by reference to the history of the early church and then by specific application to the General Missionary Society which he felt was guilty of abuses:

"There is a deep and well-founded aversion in the minds of our brethren to building up in our midst a great ecclesiastic society, endowed and independent, such as our General Society seems anxious to become. Under this head we have not forgotten the lessons of church history. Never till the church became corrupt did she sanction the formation of these great bodies; and never did corruptions flow into the church as fast from any other sources as from these bodies. I have no faith in them, but an abiding fear that they will prove the curse of the Reformation, as they did the curse of the primitive church.

"The General Society has already shown itself willing to transcend the limits of its constitution, and to become in a measure a partisan and political institution, and to control other interests and perform other acts than those contemplated in its organization. This has caused brethren to distrust it and to lose confidence in it." [13]

Restoration history has repeatedly demonstrated the propensity of societies to expand their authority to create a denominational structure. One has but to look at the International Convention of the Disciples and the United Christian Missionary Society to observe the acknowledged denomination they have created. The tentacles of state societies have reached in the same direction.

In 1913 the Wisconsin legislature passed a law at the request of the Wisconsin Christian Missionary Association designed to provide an arrangement whereby the society could assume control of property of defunct churches. The law, still on the statute books, states:

"Whenever any local religious society of the **denomination** known as the Church of Christ or the Christian Church, shall become defunct or be dissolved, the property thereof shall vest in the Wisconsin Christian Missionary Association, the state institution of said **denomination** . . . . The provisions of section 1996 shall not apply to or affect religious societies of the **denomination** known as the Church of Christ or the Christian Church." [14]

While the application of **denomination** to the churches in Wisconsin might be excused as legal terminology, the terms **Church of Christ** and **Christian Church** are obviously used in a sectarian way. Whether calling the Wisconsin Christian Missionary Association "the state institution of said denomination" is intended to imply subservance of the churches to the society or indicates that the association is the creature of the churches, there is no way to escape the implication that the law, created at the behest of the association, is talking about a denomination. No such statute would ever have been written without the request and concurrence of those directly involved.

Note that the statutes originally drawn did not exempt any congregation known locally as "Church of Christ" or "Christian Church" with no prior relationship with the state association. Legally the society was empowered to take over the property of defunct churches totally unrelated to it. This deficiency was corrected by a 1949 amendment which stipulated that the provision would be limited to any church

" . . . which accepts the Wisconsin Christian Missionary Association as its missionary organization." [15]

It may be reasoned that since a defunct church cannot function, someone has to take care of the matter. Often this is provided for by the church itself in stipulating that its assets will be conveyed to a sister congregation in the event of its demise. But the unilateral action of a missionary society in taking over the place of worship of a defunct congregation is denominational to the core. It would be hard to deny that in so doing it has not assumed a denominational prerogative. While not all actions of similar organizations are so well defined as this, it is apparent that most societies do assume rights properly residing in the congregation. To the degree that they so act they are denominational.

Of course, the assumption of congregational rights by such bodies is frequently with the agreement of the churches themselves. This does not eliminate the denominational nature of the action any more than the banding together of a group of Baptist congregations for joint endeavor erases their denominational status because the initiative was voluntary.

The tendency of the missionary society to usurp congregational authority is summed up by J. D. Thomas:

"What we mean by 'control,' is that the Missionary Society is an organization whose board 'legislates,' or passes rules that they expect to be binding upon the member churches, and where the member churches expect to be so bound. The society chooses for, directs, assesses contributions, and legislates; all of which are binding and obligatory upon the member churches. **The will of the church is subservient to the will of the society**; both the churches and the society understand that this is to be the arrangement, and therefore the member churches have surrendered their autonomy—they no longer have self-government or

122

the right of self-government. The Society dominates the churches, can coerce them and can bring authoritative, **organic** pressure upon them if they do not live up to the demands which the Society makes of them. The churches are expected to do **all** of their mission work through the Society and to do **none** of their own planning. When they join the Society they surrender fully all rights of any kind toward planning their own mission work and toward exercising any control of any kind over it in the administration." [16]

In fairness to the societies it should be observed that these conclusions do not always follow. In 1953 the Wisconsin Christian Missionary Association had emerged from a battle with the unified promotion of the Disciples from which it withdrew in 1947 when it determined to chart an independent course. Through its publication it issued a disclaimer of any action that would rob congregations of their autonomy.

"The Wisconsin Christian Missionary Association is an association or society of individuals who have applied for membership as is described in article three of the constitution. There is no provision made in the constitution for membership on any other basis, thus no collective group can be a member as such, nor does any member maintain any representative or delegate status. Each individual member may represent only himself and has the power of democratic vote at the annual meetings by virtue of that fact . . . . The Wisconsin Christian Missionary Association is not affiliated with any organization or agency. The association exists solely for the purpose of promoting the cause of New Testament Christianity in Wisconsin . . . . The association does not preclude the possibility of any local congregation from doing any missionary work which it wants to do in the state, in fact, it would encourage such vision and work . . . . The association does not nor can it assume the initiative or primary function of the local church." [17]

On the face of it this statement removes this organization from denominational status so long as its actions are consistent with the declaration. Counterbalancing this, of course, is the 1913 Wisconsin statute previously alluded to which remains law.

What has been said of missionary societies can also be applied to other organizations which might intrude upon local church autonomy. Colleges or publishing houses can conceivably become denominational organizations by assuming the decision making role for the congregation. It has sometimes been charged that subtle political pressures have been applied to congregations by

123

religious papers or colleges to make them conform to the "party line." If true, this would be a form of sectarianism even though the denominational legal structure was not present.

In summary, whether an organization is a denominational expression of a group of churches is determined by the function it fulfills, not its title. If it receives from congregations, but does not determine their policies, it is not denominational on that basis, although its biblical right to exist may be challenged. But if it helps to mold the actions of the churches and in so doing diminishes their autonomy, it becomes to that extent a denominational organization and they partake of that sectarianism.

## FOOTNOTES

1. Joseph Franklin and J. A. Headington, **The Life and Times of Benjamin Franklin** (St. Louis: John Burns, 1879), pp. 303, 304.

2. Charles Alexander Young, **Historical Documents Advocating Christian Union** (Chicago: Christian Century, 1904), pp. 23-25.

3. R. L. and J. W. Roberts, "Like Fire in Dry Stubble—The Stone Movement 1804 - 1832 (Part II)," **Restoration Quarterly**, Vol. 8, No. 1, First Quarter, 1965, pp. 30 - 34.

4. **Ibid.**, p. 31.

5. **Ibid.**, p. 31.

6. A. S. Hayden, **Early History of the Disciples in the Western Reserve, Ohio** (Cincinnati: Chase and Hall, 1876), p. 26.

7. **Ibid.**, p. 60.

8. T. M. Henley, "Co-operation of churches," **Millennial Harbinger**, July, 1836, pp. 333, 334.

9. Earl Irwin West, **The Search for the Ancient Order**, (Nashville, Tennessee: Gospel Advocate, 1949), Vol. 1, p. 212.

10. Franklin and Headington, **Op. Cit.**, p. 308.

11. **Ibid.**, p. 341.

12. Moses E. Lard, "Missionary Societies and Our Hymn Book," **Lard's Quarterly**, January, 1865, p. 138.

13. Moses E. Lard, "Cooperation of Missionary Societies," **Lard's Quarterly**, July, 1865, p. 445.

14. "Property of Defunct Socieites," **Wisconsin Statutes**, 1913, Chapter 91, Section 2001-9a.

15. "Property of Defunct Socieites," **Wisconsin Statutes**, 1949, 187.11.

16. J. D. Thomas, **We Be Brethren**, pp. 141, 142.

17. "A Mission in Your State With a Purpose," **Wisconsin Christian**, September, 1953, pp. 1, 2.

# CHAPTER 10
# THE PROBLEM
## OF IDENTIFICATION

One of the most perplexing aspects of undenominational Christianity is the problem of identification. Identification is important in every life, and even if we wished to escape it, we could not. We not only have names, but other forms of identification as well. A social security number is almost a necessity. If you try to cash a check in a place where you are unknown you are asked to produce a driver's license or credit cards. Identification is essential if we are to exist in an interrelated world, and while we may resent today's computerization, a return to "the good old days" would not eliminate its necessity.

In religion we must also have identification. The very name Christian is a means of designating one's faith. Identification helps the world to properly place us in its scheme of things, and assists Christians in their mutual relations.

However, the importance of being identified by the world has probably been overstressed. The signs in front of our places of worship and our advertisements in the newspaper testify to our desire to be known by those whom we seek to influence for Christ. Churches place their names on tracts, list themselves in telephone books, and communicate with the general public by means of radio and television. Most religious broadcasts make an effort to identify a specific group of people with the message being taught.

Yet, it is scarcely necessary that others know our history or that we have a denominational appellation for us to teach them.

127

The true image of the church in the eyes of the world is not the building in which it worships or the advertising campaign it carries on. Rather, it is the personal lives of the people who compose it. The most effective means of teaching is the godly life and the example of a dedicated child of God. A person may desire to become a part of "that group of Christians" because he sees in them what he wishes he had. He may be totally unfamiliar with such terms as "church of Christ," and whether there are ten or ten thousand similar congregations elsewhere is not relative to his needs. In fact, sometimes it is easier to communicate the undenominational plea if one is totally ignorant of the existence of other congregations. This is especially true where prejudices have been formed and a sectarian image implanted in the mind of the one being taught.

It is interesting that in the first century it was several decades before the Romans understood the differences between Christians and Jews. Because the religion of Jesus was built on a Jewish foundation and most early Christians were Jews, the governing authorities regarded them as another Jewish sect and accorded them the privileges granted to the Jews as a special people. Gallio, proconsul of Achaia, treated a dispute between Paul and the Jews as a family squabble (Acts 18:12-17). It was only toward the end of the first century when the Romans seem to have awakened to the reality of the situation that Christianity came to be regarded as an illegal religion, which it was not if it was just another sect of Judaism. There is not recorded in the New Testament any concerted effort on the part of Christians to correct the erroneous impression, nor do we gather that the indistinct identification made by the pagan world constituted a major problem.

Identification is more important where intercongregational relations are involved, even more so today than in apostolic times. Christians travel from one place to another for purposes of business and pleasure, and desire to locate an assembly of New Testament disciples. Many move to other localities and search for those who share their faith with whom they may cast their lot. Practically speaking, some form of identification becomes essential.

An examination of the New Testament reveals several matters pertaining to identification. The most obvious is the term applied to followers of Jesus. "And in Antioch the disciples were for the first time called Christians" (Acts 11:26). Were it not for the sectarianism of the religious world this would perhaps be sufficient identification today, but since this term has been appropriated by those of every stripe and hue, further clarification of the name "Christian" is needed.

The battle over circumcision in the primitive church was an identification problem. The Judaizing party wanted Gentiles who accepted Jesus to be identified as proselyte Jews. Probably they regarded the uncircumcision of Gentile Christians as a threat to their own Jewishness. They were actually creating a sect within the church of God over a matter of identification.

Jesus suggests one criterion for distinguishing His disciples. "A new commandment I give to you, that you love one another; even as I have loved you, that you also love one another. By this all men will know that you are my disciples, if you have love for one another" (John 13:34, 35). Before we conclude that the mutual love of Christ's disciples is too subjective a test for identification purposes, we ought to note the impact that such obvious love has on searchers for truth. Conversely, is there anything which so quickly turns one away from the Lord as the exhibition of a spirit of bitterness toward one's fellow Christians? It should still be true that simple followers of our Lord are known by the love they have for one another.

The early Christians used letters of recommendation as an aid when traveling. Paul inquires, "Are we beginning to commend ourselves again? Or do we need, as some do, letters of recommendation to you, or from you?" (2 Corinthians 3:1). These letters served as credentials and were helpful in avoiding the acceptance of false teachers. The Ephesian brethren used such a letter on behalf of Apollos when the latter was going into Achaia (Acts 18:24-28). Yet, such letters must have had their limitations, even as they do now. Unless one personally knows the letter writer, he cannot be sure of the veracity of the testimony.

John poses the problem of identification in his first epistle. "Brethren, do not believe every spirit, but test the spirits to see whether they are of God . . . . every spirit which confesses that Jesus Christ has come in the flesh is of God, and every spirit which does not confess Jesus is not of God. This is the spirit of antichrist, of which you heard that it was coming, and now it is in the world already" (1 John 4:1-3). John felt some means was necessary to separate the true disciple from the false teacher. Gnosticism was affecting the church and since the gnostics denied that Jesus had come in the flesh, John gives the simple confession that Jesus had come in the flesh as a way of marking the false prophet.

The rise of heresies at the close of the apostolic period called for measures for combatting error. One method was the concentration of power in the hands of a few bishops who could effectively handle the heretic. Thus Ignatius of Antioch in the early years of the second century continually stressed the importance of "the bishop." Typical is a comment addressed to the church at Smyrna:

"Let no man do aught of things pertaining to the Church apart from the bishop. Let that be held a valid eucharist which is under the bishop or one to whom he shall have committed it. Wheresoever the bishop shall appear, there let the people be; even as where Jesus may be, there is the universal Church. It is not lawful apart from the bishop either to baptize or to hold a love-feast; but whatsoever he shall approve, this is well-pleasing also to God; that everything which ye do may be sure and valid.

"It is reasonable henceforth that we wake to soberness, while we have (still) time to repent and turn to God. It is good to recognize God and the bishop. He that honoreth the bishop is honored of God; he that doeth aught without the knowledge of the bishop rendereth service to the devil."[1]

From this statement, written a few years after the death of the Apostle John several deductions may be made. First, the primitive system of church government under the guidance of a plurality of elders, as seen in Paul's writings, seems to have undergone a major change in a remarkably short time. Second, the exaltation of the bishop, at least in the area where Ignatius lived, was already well on its way early in the second century. Third, the beginning of apostolic succession, so important in Catholicism, is here strongly suggested—you can do nothing without the bishop. And fourth, and this is not quite so clear, the danger of heresy and the necessity of guarding the faith, was the rationale for the elevation of the bishop to a position of such prominence.

It was this danger of false teaching that gave rise to the early Christian creeds. The necessity of identifying the orthodox Christian, as contrasted with the false teacher, prompted the composition of the so-called Apostles' Creed. This creed had several forms and seems to have undergone an evolution. The earliest expression is known as the Old Roman Symbol. Most of us would probably agree with the content of this early confession, although the right of any human being to write an "official" expression of truth is quite another matter. In any event, creeds soon became a major method of distinguishing the true Christian from the purveyor of error.

In the post-apostolic period we also discover drawings of the fish as a symbol of the Christian. The first letters of each Greek word in the phrase, "Jesus Christ, God's Son, Savior," formed an acrostic spelling the word for fish, **ichthys**. Everett Ferguson suggests that it is an open question whether the initial letters of the words of the formula was the beginning of the fish symbol for Christ or whether the symbol prompted the acrostic.[2] Nevertheless, many inscriptions of the fish have been found. An epitaph discovered in a third century cemetery of S. Piette l'Estrier, Autun, reads, "Divine offspring of the heavenly Fish, preserve a reverent heart when thou takest the drink of immortality that is given among mortals."[3] While this symbol was perhaps effective in identifying Christians to one another in a day of persecution, it would hardly be helpful in an age in which we face other difficulties.

The problem of identification in the apostolic and post-apostolic periods was first, that of distinguishing the Christian from the pagan or Jew, and second, that of separating the orthodox from the heretic. Denominationalism was unknown and the mere fact that one was a faithful Christian insured his identification with fellow disciples.

We face a completely different problem today. Most people in the Western World who make a religious profession claim to be Christians. Among the multitude of denominational voices, how can one who professes to be just a Christian find those who share his faith? And how can a congregation made up of **Christians only** convey to religious neighbors that it has no association with any sectarian system? Does the fact that such a group is separate from others make it denominational?

G. C. Brewer states the dilemma facing undenominational Christians:

"But if we group undenominational Christians, separate them into a party and distinguish them from other Christians, have we not made them a denomination? Yes, indeed, and in that sense we are denominational and we must admit it. But it is not our fault. We are forced to it. We are forced to be denominational by reason of the fact that we are undenominational. I can illustrate that this way: Let us suppose that we have on this desk a great heap of cards. Some of the cards are stamped with figures, 2, 4, 6, 8, etc., and there is a great number of them that are unstamped—

131

have no figures on them. I am set to the task of separating these cards and classifying them. I place the 'twos' in one stack, the 'fours' in another stack, the 'sixes' in still another stack and so on until I have stacked all the different numbers in separate stacks; and then I have a stack of cards that we would call nondescript—unstamped cards. They are a stack of cards just as much as the others are. But let us give to the cards human intelligence and place in them the purpose that we have as Christians and we will witness a great debate. A card from the stack of 'fours' arises and says, 'Here you fanatical and inconsistent fellows, you claim to be unstamped and unstacked and yet you are bunched, stacked and classified as much as any of us.' Then a card from the nondescript bunch arises in his righteous indignation and vehemently denies. He says, 'We are not classified. We are not a stack of cards. We are just cards.' But they are a stack of cards, as you can see. They are forced to be in a stack to themselves because the others are separated into stacks and left them alone. They are classified by reason of the fact that they are unclassified. It is not their purpose to be a separate and distinct division of cards. They think that all cards ought to be just cards and all be stacked together in one big stack, but these other cards are all stamped with different figures and are therefore distinguished from one another and from those unstamped. The stamp differentiates them and that forces the unstamped cards to be **classed** as unclassified or else be stamped and go into different stacks, and they know that they can never all be one stack as long as they are separated into different classes.

"You can all see the application. It is in this sense that we are denominational. We are forced to be a separate body of people because we are undenominational; because we will not have put upon us the party names, marks and brands of the different denominations. We want the fellowship of all of God's people and we will affiliate with anybody in anything the Bible sanctions, but we can not have the fellowship of our denominational brethren without going into their peculiar and several denominations. We are therefore left in the predicament of being a separate people by virtue of the fact that we are undenominational . . . . If we are denominational then it is because our purposes and work as a body of Christians—undenominational Christians, simply Christians, Christians only—make it necessary for us to labor apart from the denominations or else become members of some one or different denominations and thus perpetuate divisions." [4]

Actually, our problem is the same that men have always faced when they have sought to emerge from denominationalism to return to God's word as their sole religious authority. There have been many indigenous movements in various lands seeking the restoration of apostolic Christianity. Each of them has encountered the same problem of identification.

Some groups have sought to exist without any name identification. The Christadelphians (Brothers of Christ) began in the 1840's under the leadership of Dr. John Thomas, an early preacher in the Restoration Movement. Not until 1864 during the Civil War did they formally adopt a name, and then its choice was dictated by their conscientious objection to participation in war and the requirement of a name in order to secure military exemption.

Those people who have been dubbed "Two-by-twos" because of their insistence on going from place to place by twos as commanded by Jesus in the Limited Commission have rejected any specific designation. This has not, however, kept others from calling them "Cooneyites" and "Go-Preachers." It is noteworthy that the world usually insists on attaching its own name if a group of people refuses to identify itself.

The Plymouth Brethren also present an interesting study of a group that has sought to be undenominational. Their name is not of their choosing nor with their approval. While they call themselves "brethren," the designation "Plymouth Brethren" was attached to them by others because one of their early assemblies was located in Plymouth, England. Their history dates to about 1830. Common influences with the Restoration Movement may be traced, particularly in the Haldanes who influenced the early thinking of Alexander Campbell. However, in their inception the two efforts were completely independent except for their similar principles. The Plymouth Brethren are immersionists and akin to the Baptists in teaching relating to salvation. They are also dispensationalists. They have fractured into several elements, the most important known as "Exclusive Brethren" and "Open Brethren."

Because they profess to be undenominational, these people have refrained from adopting any exclusive descriptive term. Their places of worship are variously called "Gospel Chapel," "Good News Chapel," "Bible Chapel," or "Community Chapel." The "Open Brethren" have a directory of congregations as an aid to travelers. While they readily acknowledge that disciples of Jesus may be scripturally called "brethren," "believers," "saints," or "Christians," they employ the phrase "Christians gathered unto the name of the Lord" as a means of designating those who share their faith. This expression seems to be a code as was the fish among early Christians or similar phrases largely used by those in the Restoration Movement. The Plymouth Brethren have faced the same problems of identification as has the Restoration Movement, but apparently have had greater success in maintaining an undenominational image. Their comparative numerical smallness is undoubtedly a factor since the world is less inclined to label the insignificant, but their refusal to employ any exclusive designation has also contributed to their undenominational posture.

The problem in the Restoration Movement has not been so much the use of unscriptural terminology for identification purposes as the unscriptural use of scriptural terminology. True, there have been numerous articles written on the pros and cons of "Christian Church" as applied to the body of Christ. But the root difficulty has been that of taking an acknowledged biblical term such as "Church of Christ" and misusing it. Most of us can readily see that when a group calling itself the "Church of God" puts "Anderson, Indiana," in parenthesis after those words it has completed the process of denominationalizing an otherwise scriptural designation. Were it not that there is another group of people similarly describing itself with headquarters in Cleveland, Tennessee, it is unlikely that they would add the parenthetical phrase. They feel it incumbent that they be distinguished from others and so to a biblical term they add a denominational epithet. But what about those congregations whose highway signs advertise, "Church of Christ—Vocal Music"? The obvious purpose of this identification is to make a distinction from churches using instrumental music. Or what about those congregations in the latter category whose signs proclaim, "Church of Christ (Christian)"? Such a phrase is designed as an appeal to those whose home congregations may be known either as "Church of Christ" or "Christian Church." They are concerned that failure to put both expressions on their house of worship will cause some to go astray. Both of these uses are clearly denominational and illustrate how biblical phraseology can be misused.

Much of the problem relates to the exclusive use of a single term as a designation of assemblies of Christ. How do you find a congregation sharing your faith when you are in a strange community? The average person will consult the telephone directory or newspaper. He will look for "Church of Christ," beneath which he discovers the places of meeting of those advertising under this name. If he has questions about the scripturality of the group he plans to visit, a phone call can establish the doctrinal position of the church in question. Probably he will simply visit on Sunday and by the way the worship is conducted draw his own conclusions as to whether he is in the right pew.

Let us suppose that as he drives through the city he sees a sign reading, "Church of Jesus Christ." "Mormon," he would likely comment, even though "Latter Day Saints" might not be on the sign. But is it not as scriptural to refer to the body of Jesus as the church of Jesus Christ as to call it the church of Christ? Why should the name meaning "Savior" turn us off? Is it not that because we have never seen it done this way we conclude we have found the wrong church? Why not call it the church of God? The usual response is, "Then we would be confused with one of the Pentecostal groups because that's the name they wear." This is probably true. However, we must ask in all honesty if that is a sufficient reason to reject a biblical term.

"But what would happen," someone inquires, "if all congregations did not wear a uniform name? Would we ever be able to find another congregation?" Doubtless the task would be more difficult, although the very exercise would likely impress upon us the undenominational nature of Christ's church. In the long run it might be better.

If we still have difficulty in seeing the fallacy of using a single expression, even a biblical one, to designate a congregation of believers, the following examples should put the matter into focus:

"This business of trying to monopolize on the name of the church can run into some rather curious developments. I heard of one town where a church which called itself the 'Church of God' had split and the dissenters went over to the other side of town and called their church the 'True Church of God.' Later on this latter group divided and the splinter group went to another location and called itself the 'Only True Church of God'! While some might laugh at such, yet is it any more ridiculous than how 'Church of Christ' is used in many places today?

"I heard about another congregation, a group of Negro worshipers down in the red clay hill country of north Georgia, who also wanted to make sure they had an exclusive name. Over the door of their unpainted clapboard sided building, they scrawled a sign reading, 'The Church of the New Jerusalem—the One John Saw Coming Right Down Out of Heaven.' One could hardly beat that for being exclusively specific!" 5

M. C. Kurfees went to the heart of the matter when he wrote:

"The wrong here is not in using some one of the divinely authorized designations of the church, for this is entirely proper at any and all times, but it is in rejecting all the rest from usage . . . . And yet this is rapidly becoming a fixed habit in some places. The name, or designation, 'the church of Christ,' is coming to be used, in some sections of the country, to the exclusion of every other New Testament designation of the church." [6]

Some object to having "Church of Christ" attached to a place of worship on the ground that the church is the people, not the building. It is better, they feel, to write, "The Church of Christ Meets Here." If a congregation chooses to employ this expression there can be no objection. But let us recognize that words are simply vehicles of communications. When you see "First Baptist Church" or "Calvary Presbyterian Church" in front of places of worship, do you not think of the people rather than the edifice? Those words identify the congregation, not the structure. Similarly, to the average person "Church of Christ" on the sign in front of the building conveys the thought, "The people who worship here are known as the Church of Christ." The problem is not confusing the building with the people, but confusing the people with a denomination.

There is no simple solution to the problem of identifying undenominational Christians. Some have suggested using **chapel** to designate the place of meeting as a chapel is a place of worship. Thus it is proposed that the sign might read, "Walnut Street Chapel—A congregation of Christians meets here for worship."[7] This proposal has value and would likely convey the undenominational concept. This is essentially what the Plymouth Brethren have done.

Another suggestion is worthy of serious consideration. Some years ago F. G. Allen carried on a discussion with some Methodists in Louisville. An article was published in **The Central Methodist** and quoted by Allen in **The Old Path Guide.** It contains a tongue in cheek suggestion that should be considered:

"Let us give this church a little advice. Call yourselves 'The Church.' This is a Scriptural name, and you feel that way, and if your people take a little pride in the title, let them enjoy it." [8]

The suggestion has merit. Why cannot individual congregations simply be identified by such terms as "Main Street Church" or "Northside Church"? In the eyes of the world this would mark such an assembly of disciples as undenominational, giving credibility to its claim.

"But," you inquire, "how could one find a faithful congregation when going to another city?" Since most people consult the yellow pages of the telephone book or the weekend listing in the newspaper, those congregations made up of **Christians only** could be listed under the heading of "Undenominational" or "Nondenominational." To use G. C. Brewer's illustration, one would simply look among the "unclassified cards."

One of the strongest advocates in his time of the undenominational plea was M. C. Kurfees who served the Haldeman Avenue Church in Louisville, Kentucky, as evangelist for forty-five years. Kurfees believed that in designating itself simply as "the church" a congregation could more clearly set forth its undenominational stance. Through his influence the Campbell Street Church advertised in the newspaper as "Campbell Street Church, Campbell between Main and Market Streets." While Kurfees recognized that such a designation did not fully describe the congregation, he argued that the identification was not misleading as might be true if it were known as "the church of Christ" which in the minds of some would classify it as a sect. [9] When a new place of worship on Haldeman Avenue was erected, the same approach was used and for fifty years the congregation was called the "Haldeman Avenue Church." However, early in 1974 the congregation offically adopted the name "Haldeman Avenue Church of Christ," concluding a noble experiment in the interest of undenominational Christianity. In our opinion this was a major step backward brought about, no doubt, by the pressures to conform to the practices of other Christian assemblies.

The pressure which society exerts upon Christians to compel conformity to its standards is immense. That is why Paul enjoins us in Romans 12:2, "Adapt yourselves no longer to the pattern of this present world." (N.E.B.) If we are to exalt the distinctive principles of apostolic Christianity, then undenominational Christians must have the courage to free themselves from the fetters of sectarian thought and to express themselves to the world in such a way that this undenominational plea cannot be misunderstood.

# FOOTNOTES

1. Ignatius, "Epistle to the Smyrnaeans," J. B. Lightfoot, **The Apostolic Fathers** (Grand Rapids, Michigan: Baker Book House, 1970), p. 84.

2. Everett Ferguson, **Early Christians Speak** (Austin, Texas: Sweet, 1971), p. 42.

3. Henry Bettenson, **Documents of the Christian Church** (London: Oxford University Press, 1967), p. 86.

4. G. C. Brewer, **Murfreesboro Addresses** (Cincinnati: F. L. Rowe, 1917), pp. 161, 162.

5. Talmadge F. McNabb, "The Church With the Right Name," **Sentinel of Truth,** Vol. 4, No. 4, October, 1968.

6. M. C. Kurfees, "Bible Things by Bible Names—Different Designations of the Church Further Considered," **Gospel Advocate,** September 30, 1920, p. 959.

7. W. Carl Ketcherside, "That They All May be One," **Mission Messenger,** January, 1957, p. 3.

8. Anonymous, "What Is Their Name?", **The Old Path Guide,** February, 1880, p. 59.

9. M. C. Kurfees, **Op Cit.,** p. 959.

# CHAPTER 11
# "ARE 'WE' A DENOMINATION?"

"Viewed either sociologically or scripturally, the Church of Christ is not the church of Christ. Its members, in a sense, are neither 'Christians only' nor 'the only Christians.' Its fragmentation cancels out the first proposition. The arrogance of the second displays an attitude wholly contrary to the genius of Christianity." [1]

The above quotation is from one of seventeen essays published in 1966 purporting to be "critical studies in Church of Christism." Throughout the book runs the theme that "the Churches of Christ should admit the reality of their denominational status . . . . " [2] These statements give one answer to the question so frequently asked among those in the Restoration Movement, "Are 'we' a denomination?"

The response to our question will depend largely upon who is making the evaluation. It will also be governed by one's definition of "we" and the meaning attached to "denomination." Before seeking a definitive answer we should again define the undenominational church in the biblical sense:

"The church Christ built includes all the saved; and it includes no one else. There is not one saved who is not in it. There is not one in it who is not saved. The guarantee of this is that the same one does both the saving and the adding to the church. The church is the saved." [3]

The church of God is not identical to the Restoration Movement. To assume an identity would require that the sinner be taught by someone associated with that effort before he could become a Christian. Few will make this contention. Christ's body is larger than any movement within it, regardless of its doctrinal stance or spiritual stature. This is not to imply, however, that those with roots in the Reformation of the Nineteenth Century are denominational merely because the Lord's church is larger than the movement. The "churches of Galatia" (Galatians 1:2) were not a sect, even though collectively they were not the sum total of the universal body.

When Isaac Errett inquired editorially in 1878 if "we" are a denomination, he undoubtedly applied the "we" to the restoration effort in its entirety. Others of that era who posed the question thought of the same people, even if they disagreed with Errett's position. Unfortunately, division has since troubled the movement begun by the Campbells and Stone. To a modern "Disciple" the "we" would designate that body known officially as the Christian Church (Disciples of Christ). To one associated with the more conservative "independent" congregations it would likely denote those in that fellowship. This is made clear by the **Directory of the Ministry of the Undenominational Fellowship of Christian Churches and Churches of Christ** which specifically excludes both the Disciples and those "churches of Christ" which do not use instruments in worship. [4] To those in most "non-instrumental" congregations "we" would refer to those embracing the position generally shared by them. In some cases the "we" would be much smaller, being limited, perhaps, to those who agree that individual communion cups and Bible classes are wrong, or to those who oppose children's homes or certain kinds of congregational cooperation. It would, in fact, be virtually impossible to find anyone who would apply the "we" to all the living heirs of the Restoration Movement and still affirm that the movement as an entity is not a denomination. It is more realistic, therefore, to inquire whether **some** of the churches in the Campbell-Stone tradition are truly undenominational.

One response to the question under consideration is what may be called the sociological answer. For the average person there is little difference between a sect and a denomination. Sociologists, however, attach different values to the terms **church, denomination,** and **sect** than are current in popular usage. These meanings are part of a social theory pioneered by Ernst Troeltsch and others in the early twentieth century and modified by later writers. The theory affirms that a religious group begins as a sect and over a period of time evolves into a church or denomination. This is called the "sect-to-denomination" process. The word **church** (or **ecclesiastical body**) designates those national European churches which grew out of the Protestant Reformation, such as the Church of England or the various state Lutheran churches of Germany and Scandinavia. The **denomination** is the independent body with many of the sociological characteristics of the European national churches, but without the church-state relationship. Most larger non-Catholic groups in the Americas fall into this category and in this part of the world the denomination is considered normative. **Sect** is applied to the more exclusive group which refuses to be pressed into the mold of society and which is often an offshoot of an established church or denomination against which it has revolted.

This sociological theory asserts that initially the sect is characterized by moral strictness and rigid biblical literalism. It believes it has the truth. Consequently it refuses to compromise its views and tends to isolate itself from association with other religious bodies. It appeals to the poor and reflects the attitudes of the socially disinherited. The sect expresses the social needs of a particular group of people and its doctrinal attitudes are colored by the culture of its members. In time, however, it tends to moderate its views as it accommodates itself to society. As a better educated and more affluent generation replaces the group's pioneers, there is a loss of militancy, a desire to be recognized by others, and a striving for the "better things of life." The sect has now become a denomination. It is more willing to tolerate its religious neighbors, and while as a sect it was primarily interested in the individual, it is now concerned with the betterment of society. It tends to reflect the attitudes of society and even borrows its ethics from the community. Doctrine is less important than in the sect and a diminution of dedication to the early principles of the effort is apparent.

Not all groups fit neatly into any of these sociological categories. The term **institutionalized-sect** is applied to those extreme groups which, developing institutionally in much the same way as the denomination, retain a distinctive character keeping them out of the denominational mainstream. The Mormons would fall into this classification.

Using the sociological definition one would have to conclude that the early church was a sect. It appealed to the downtrodden, was militant in its message and uncompromising with its neighbors in its moral attitudes. Although its views leavened society, its plea was directed to the individual and the salvation of his soul. Such social causes as the removal of slavery were not

141

considered of first importance. From virtually every point of view it would be classified sociologically as a sect. Perhaps we should not be surprised that some of the Jews in Rome declared of the church, "But we desire to hear from you what your views are; for with regard to this **sect** we know that everywhere it is spoken against" (Acts 28:22). However, the primitive church was not a sect according to the ordinary definition. It was, in fact, the body of Christ, and a redefinition of terms does not alter the fact.

Several writers have examined the Restoration Movement in the sociological context. The earliest, and one of the most definitive, is W. E. Garrison's **Religion Follows the Frontier.** More recent writings include **Trumpet Call of Reformation** by Oliver Read Whitley and **Quest for a Christian America** by David Edwin Harrell, Jr. [5] Harrell, in his booklet, **Emergence of the 'Church of Christ' Denomination,** concludes that at least some of the Disciples of Christ have completed the sect-to-denomination process. He declares:

"Liberal Disciples today are, by and large, proud to have made the transition to denominationalism, and have gained new insight into the meaning of the restoration movement." [6]

The main thesis of Harrell's booklet is that the more conservative element in the Restoration Movement is also currently undergoing the sect-to-denomination process. His analysis is:

"What had happened by the middle of the twentieth century was simply the completion of the 'sect to denomination' cycle again—the familiar process constantly at work in American religious history. In the course of the half-century since 1900 one segment of the membership of the church had grown wealthier, better educated, and more sophisticated. This new generation of 'Church of Christers' (largely the children and grandchildren of the pioneers who lived around the turn of the century) has reached the sociological status which demands a more denominational expression of Christianity. The old values of the early leaders of the movement are no longer an acceptable expression of Christianity to this sophisticated element. By 1960, the most liberal element within the church was well on its way into the mainstream of American denominationalism.

"On the other hand, in this schism, as in the divisions of the past, it was not the entire church which made the transition. A substantial minority—the fervent and generally the less affluent classes—retained the old attitudes about religion. They yet refuse to make the transition and remain committed to the conservative theological standards which fit their religious presuppositions." [7]

There is some truth in Harrell's appraisal. Far too many in the conservative element of the Restoration Movement have lost the earnest convictions of their forbears and have become increasingly concerned about status in the eyes of their neighbors. Frequently the focus of attention has been upon notable personalities in the sports, entertainment, and business worlds as a means of declaring to society, "Look who we are!" Perhaps it is providential that some of these people have proved to be sources of embarrassment, thus demonstrating that we should reflect the light of Jesus rather than basking in the aura of fellow human beings. The great stress upon bigger and more expensive places of worship as churches have crossed the tracks to assume their place beside the denominations causes one to wonder if the plea of back to the Bible has not become somewhat distorted. The world will be saved, not by the material impression that is made upon it, but by the simple message of the man of Galilee.

Harrell acknowledges that his convictions have influenced his conclusions. He is closely associated with Christians who oppose the method of congregational cooperation practiced by some others, and the "substantial minority" which has "retained the old attitudes about religion" is this group of brethren. Of course, those with differing doctrinal positions would disagree with him as to who walks in the "old paths." People of earnest conviction stand where they are because they believe they are right. If honest they will alter their stance when convinced they are wrong.

The sociological answer to the question, "Are 'we' a denomination?" requires that those in the restoration effort be either a sect or denomination, or somewhere in between. Sociologists would classify the early Restoration Movement as a sect, and those who stand substantially in the position of the early leaders would be in this same category. The more liberal element is, by its own acknowledgement, sociologically denominational, while others would more accurately be represented by the institutionalized-sect classification.

The sociological approach has validity as a means of explaining developments within religious bodies. Economic status and cultural attitudes do bear upon theological views. For example, contrast the Pentecostal and Christian Science churches and note how differences in education and economic well-being of their members have been reflected in their spiritual attitudes and cultures.

However, undue reliance on the sect-to-denomination explanation can easily depreciate the importance of doctrine as the basic explanation of historical development in the Restoration Movement. Few similar reformatory efforts have placed such stress on a "thus saith the Lord" for every religious practice. The traditional explanation that differences in biblical interpretation have caused the divisions that have occurred is still valid. Thus, Christians have gone their separate ways because they honestly could not agree about how to worship or how the church should be structured or how Christ is going to return. Sociology affords an insight into those factors which have helped mold men's attitudes toward the scriptures, but any explanation that fails to recognize the importance of doctrine in the Restoration Movement is inadequate.

The major weakness of the sociological explanation is that it attaches different meanings to words that convey distinct ideas to the average person. It is safe to say that the average individual never heard of the sociological definitions. The popular abridged dictionaries do not include them, and while this does not invalidate their use in the proper context, it is very misleading to answer a theological question with sociological terms given altered definitions. To say that sociologists regard the church as a sect or a denomination is an improper response to the question raised.

Furthermore, there is no room in the sociological perspective for undenominational Christianity. By definition a non-Catholic who professes to be a Christian must be a member of either a sect or a denomination. To be just a Christian is not even possible. So while the sociological explanation is valuable in interpreting religious development, it cannot answer the question, "Are 'we' a denomination?" For this a biblical answer must be found.

But the charge of denominationalism in the Restoration Movement issues from sources other than sociologists. It is reflected in the views expressed at the beginning of this chapter. A well-known editor states his thinking in this way:

"The religious institution commonly called 'The Church of Christ' of which you are members, and of which many are preachers, is not a restoration of the primitive church of God, but is a twentieth century sect growing out of a non-sectarian restoration movement of the previous century, now employing all the means and methods of other sects, and should be regarded in that light."[8]

Similar quotations from others could be multiplied. They add up to the contention that all, or at least most, of the churches in the heritage of the Restoration Movement are sectarian. The above quoted writer cautions that there are some congregations and individuals who do not fall under his indictment. Others are not so charitable and would make a blanket condemnation. The critics range from those who have left the movement to others with a grasp of the undenominational principle. Generally, they tend to the liberal end of the restoration spectrum, although there are exceptions. Some obviously do not have a clear understanding of undenominational Christianity. It is hard to appreciate how others can be undenominational if one does not think in such terms himself.

Before immediately rejecting this allegation, it is wise to examine the various reasons assigned for charging that "we" are a denomination. It is not possible here to consider all of the charges, but they fall into about four categories. First, there are the doctrinal objections. Some view insistence on immersion and the teaching of the verbal inspiration of the scriptures as an expression of sectarianism and a barrier to the unity with affusionists and those who are unwilling to accept the full inspiration of God's word. However, it would be a surrender of principle for those who are convinced of the truthfulness of these matters to compromise in these areas. Many of the liberal "Disciples" have done this very thing and have ended up abandoning both undenominational Christianity and the restoration principle in the traditional sense.

Other doctrinal accusations are more valid. They include the indictments that the name of the church has been denomination-alized, that a pastor system which is deviant from the apostolic pattern has been established, that a legalistic approach to the scriptures has been taken, and that there have been failures in coming to grips with the real problems of life and in adequately teaching the grace of God. The misuse of biblical terminology has already been discussed. As to a "pastor" system there is undoubtedly a need to draw closer to the apostolic norm in which the elders do the shepherding while preachers of the gospel concentrate on proclamation of the word. The validity of the charge will vary from place to place, but among a people emphasizing the apostolic pattern it is proper to take another look at this aspect of primitive Christianity.

The criticisms of failing to come to grips with life's problems and a lack of stress on divine grace are justified in some congregations, but totally unwarranted in others. Unfortunately some base their conclusions on their own personal experiences and unnecessarily indict those who are not guilty.

The legitimacy of the accusation of legalism depends on the definition attached to the word. One meaning assigned to it is "close adherence to law; strict conformity to law." It is perhaps in this sense that David Edwin Harrell affirms:

"I believe that the old faith is good; I believe that the legalistic plea for the restoration of the ancient order of things is valid; and I believe that the denominational evolutions of the nineteenth and the twentieth centuries are inconsistent, unscriptural, and sinful." [9]

If by legalism one means strict adherence to the authority of God's word, many would willingly acknowledge that this is their view. They would then inquire if this is not precisely what God desires.

A second definition of legalism is "the theological doctrine of salvation by works, as distinguished from that by grace." Few in the Restoration Movement would acknowledge advocating such a teaching, and most would vehemently deny such.

Most charges of legalism, however, stem from a third meaning of the word—"the tendency to observe the letter rather than the spirit of the law." The Restoration Movement has long emphasized the importance of carrying out the commands of God. It has logically asked for scriptural proof for religious practices and has rejected those for which no such evidence was found. Sometimes, in attempting to fulfill the letter, the spirit has been overlooked. Some, especially among the smaller groups within the movement, have become "gnat strainers" in calling for a divine pattern where many feel none is required. It is unfair, however, categorically to condemn all for the mistakes of some. There are thousands of congregations whose approach to the biblical message is not legalistic.

A second group of charges relates to authoritarianism. It is contended that there is a political power system in which pressure is exerted to compel Christians to conform to the "party line." It is affirmed that true freedom in Christ cannot be found. Here again some accusations can be documented. There have, in fact, been instances of "witch hunting" in which an honest search for truth was stifled by the duress of pressure. I recall over thirty years ago being told by a young preacher then attending a Christian college that were I to go to the school I had chosen I wouldn't be able to find a place to preach! This is what he had been told where he attended. I did not heed his warning and have never wanted for a place to tell the story of Jesus, and so long as there are souls to be saved there will always be a place. The charge of authoritarianism is usually overstated, drawing on personal experiences which have embittered the accusers. An indictment which is unnecessarily broad results.

Thirdly, it is contended that attitudes among those professing to be just Christians do not conform to the spirit of Christ. Bigotry in racial matters, a "we-are-right-you-are-wrong" attitude toward other religious people, and traditionalism are all cited as examples. While "proof" can be found in all of these areas, the brush usually paints too wide a stroke and the attitudes of some are attributed to all. The specific problem of traditionalism will be dealt with in the next chapter.

Finally, it is asserted that the party spirit and the factionalism it belies are proof positive of the denominationalism of the Restoration Movement. One must be ignorant to deny that the Nineteenth Century Reformation has divided on several occasions. Yet, it does not follow that everyone involved in division is sectarian. The early church was also plagued with divisiveness. Most of us would not condemn Paul for his role in the circumcision controvery though his hard line against the Judaizers temporarily intensified the strife. To have capitulated for the sake of unity would have made the Christian faith merely an adjunct of Judaism. It is sometimes necessary to stand for what you believe is truth in spite of the division which may be engendered.

The degree of division in the Restoration Movement is sometimes overstated. Typical is this comment:

"The disciple brotherhood is fractured into more than two dozen splinter parties, each with its unwritten creed and its special tests of fellowship. Each one of these claims to be the church, whole and entire, perfect and wanting nothing; each regards the others as factions." [10]

The ability of the writer to find two dozen groups associated in some manner with the Restoration Movement can hardly be questioned. However, it should be pointed out that most of these are numerically small elements that many people have never

147

heard of. I must confess that in the enumeration of the parties listed I discovered a couple of which I was completely unaware.

Any division, however, is unfortunate. Though all are not responsible for the condition, all ought to seek the solution on the basis of divine authority and love. Some positive suggestions will be considered under the heading of fellowship.

What merit is there, then, to the charge that all or most of the churches in the Restoration Movement are denominational because of failures in the realm of doctrine, authoritarianism, attitudes, and unity? Perhaps we should take another look at the early church. In spite of its divine foundation, its human superstructure was far from perfect. The same problems which exist today existed then in slightly different forms. There were doctrinal departures at Corinth (1 Corinthians 5:1; 6:1-8; 5:12); there was sectarianism within the same congregation (1 Corinthians 1:10-12); some disciples exhibited unchristian attitudes, even bigotry (Philippians 1:15-17; James 2:1-6); and there were those such as Diotrephes who were guilty of authoritarianism (3 John 9, 10). Yet collectively this body was not a denomination. Although there may be a relationship, imperfection and denominationalism are not to be equated. At what point the Lord will declare, "Repent and do the first works; or else I come to thee, and will move thy candlestick out of its place" (Revelation 2:5—A.S.V.), we cannot know. When a congregation ceases to be the church of God only the Lord can determine. Perhaps God is more longsuffering than we. Many of us would anathematize a congregation like the one in Corinth because of division, false doctrine, and immorality, yet Paul addressed it as "the church of God which is at Corinth" (1 Corinthians 1:2).

The imperfection of those congregations which profess undenominational status does not necessarily invalidate that claim. The pen that portrays most of these churches as sectarian because of attitudes or errors displayed upon occasion unfairly indicts those thousands of fellowships which strive to belong only to Christ.

A third response to the question, "Are 'we' a denomination?" is given by those who believe that the body of Christ is circumscribed by correct doctrine. They equate the Lord's church with those who give accurate answers to a given set of doctrinal or moral questions. Those who reply correctly are in the undenominational church of Christ while those who respond erroneously are erring brethren at best or completely out of Christ at worst.

It has already been suggested that one of the characteristics of denominationalism is doctrinal error. John did not regard those first century believers who denied that Jesus is the Christ as true Christians. He even calls them the antichrist (1 John 2:18-23). There obviously is a body of essential truth which Jesus' disciple must accept to be among the saved. It is proper to compare a congregation with the apostolic model to determine if it is pleasing to God. The demands of conscience may even require that one withhold his personal fellowship from an assembly of disciples because its teachings are foreign to God's word or he cannot worship in faith according to the practices of the group.

However, those holding the view we are describing usually choose a limited group of questions as a means of determining the boundaries of the kingdom of God. The criteria for doctrinal soundness vary from group to group and often reflect current issues. Thus in wartime the Christian's participation in combat may be debated to the rupture of fellowship, while in times of peace disagreement presents no barrier to a harmonious relationship. On the other hand, matters of extreme importance which might also precipitate disagreement are often ignored.

This approach is taken by Burnell Rawls in a tract entitled, **Do I Belong to the Right Church?** He concludes that right doctrine includes opposition to individual communion cups, Bible classes, and women teachers. Interestingly he says nothing about opposition to stealing, adultery, drunkenness, lying, and murder. To him a congregation which uses multiple containers in partaking of the fruit of the vine in the Lord's supper is in error and therefore is denominational. [11]

The extremes to which this attitude leads is illustrated by a quotation from **The Warrior** of August 1, 1959, as quoted in another publication. Were it not so tragic, most of us would regard it humorously:

"Brethren: We wish to compile and publish a list of LOYAL congregations. We want to make a directory of local congregations for the benefit of the traveling brethren who wish to worship with loyal congregations: secondly, for the benefit of brethren who are desirous of moving to a loyal congregation. To compile this directory we need the following information. Describe every act of worship in your assemblies. Describe your position on the communion. Do you have one or two communions on Sunday? Do you use only one cup and loaf? Do you fellowship the Sunday School or cups brethren? Do you fellowship the Old

Paths Advocate? Or other digressives? Do you advocate any doctrine or act of worship that is called a hobby by most of the brotherhood? If you want to be counted among the honored few, give us correct answers to all of our questions, otherwise you will be left out of our directory . . . . Are you living in a state of division, having pulled off from another congregation? Please answer all questions. Do you contend that the cup must have a handle on it? Do you contend that the cup must not have a handle on it?" [12]

Frankly, the Apostle Paul would not meet the test! It is impossible to find the scripture in which he discusses whether the cup must have a handle! While this quotation will seem ridiculous to most of us, it outlines in bold relief the fallacy of selecting a group of questions, often inconsequential, as a means of determining whose names are written in the Lamb's Book of Life.

A generally well written booklet entitled, **The New Testament Church,** outlines the reasoning by which this approach is justified. Under the heading of "Its Identity," the following conclusions are drawn:

"II. Only One Religious Body Can Be Identical With the New Testament Church.

1. Every religious body bears one or more points of resemblance to the New Testament church.
2. One point of dissimilarity brands a religious body as a counterfeit of the New Testament church.
3. The Church of Christ is identical with the New Testament in every respect. It is the New Testament church." [13]

Point one is essentially correct. Point two, however, requires congregational perfection if an assembly is to be the New Testament church. It assumes there were no intercongregational differences in the first century. An examination of the Corinthian letters reveals the toleration of incest at Corinth (1 Corinthians 5:1, 2) and a denial by some of the resurrection of the dead (1 Corinthians 15:12). Assuredly all of the early churches did not fall short in these areas. Taking them as examples, "the church of God which is at Corinth" did not qualify as a New Testament church.

If the writer in defining the apostolic body refers to the New Testament ideal in contrast with the actual imperfection, no present day congregation can meet the test. At that point at which a church ceases to attain the ideal it becomes, because of this dissimilarity, a counterfeit. Many churches fall short of fulfilling the apostolic directives in the area of church discipline. Others lack the total committment to Christ evident among many early disciples. Still others have yet to grasp the urgency of taking the good news of Christ to the lost. Many of these churches are diligently striving to attain the perfection the Lord desires. Shall we conclude that until they do so their points of "dissimilarity" to the apostolic model brand them as counterfeit?

Point three states that "the Church of Christ is identical with the New Testament in every respect. It is the New Testament church." If by "the Church of Christ" the undenominational body of Christ containing all of the saved is intended, the statement is meaningless since it is in effect saying "the church is the church." On the other hand, it seems that the writer has in mind a group of existing churches associated with the Restoration Movement, smaller than the whole body of Christ, but possessing the same characteristics as the apostolic church. If this is the case, he is presuming that the absolute restoration of primitive Christianity has been achieved in every respect, that "we" have arrived and have the truth, the whole truth, and nothing but the truth. There is no room for human imperfection and no place for those disagreements found in every congregation. This line of reasoning sets an impossible standard and makes an unrealistic claim totally out of keeping with the facts.

The invalidity of the strictly doctrinal approach can be seen best when viewed in those with whom we differ rather than in ourselves. Different groups within the restoration heritage apply different tests. Reference has been made to those who elevate the standard of communion cups, classes, and women teachers. For others soundness is determined by opposition to certain kinds of congregational cooperation, children's homes, and eating in the church building. Some would proscribe those who attend moving pictures and wear make-up.

Certainly we are to "contend earnestly for the faith" (Jude 3—A.S.V.). This includes opposition to error. But do we have the right to select a few issues on which we believe we are correct and by these, to the neglect of other matters of importance, define those who are in the body of Christ? Have we not at times become guilty of majoring in minors? Is eating in the church building really more important than smoking outside it? Is there one who will self-righteously affirm that he believes no error? If absolute doctrinal agreement is a prerequisite to fellowship in the same body, we will have to have a separate congregation for

151

each Christian! Truly, one does not have to live in the time of Jesus to "tithe mint and anise and cummin and neglect the weightier matters of the law."

One mistake in the position that assumes that the undenominational body may be defined according to doctrinal accuracy is that it does not allow for the grace of God in forgiving doctrinal error. Most of us recognize that unconscious sins in the moral realm will be forgiven the Christian through the unmerited favor of a loving God. Why should God not extend that grace to those who sincerely believe, and even practice, doctrinal error? Of course, one who persists in what he knows is wrong cannot expect that God's mercy will bridge the gap between the divine standard and himself for the simple reason that he has not repented. It is the position taken here that both individual disciples and congregations can fall short of doctrinal perfection without nullifying their claim to be undenominational. Therefore, though two congregations may differ doctrinally in some respects, each may still be a part of the body of Christ, even as the Jerusalem and Corinthian churches were in the same body, though both at times tolerated erroneous views. The difference may even be so great as to preclude their working in concert without it affecting their acceptance by God.

Finally, the doctrinal test ignores the fact that denominationalism is often caused by factors other than doctrine. A congregation might be as close to truth in doctrine as humanly possible and still possess the spirit of sectarianism. Not only is the doctrinal application too narrow in that it calls for doctrinal perfection, but it is too broad because it ignores other elements of sectarianism.

A fourth approach to our question is the **brotherhood** answer. According to this view the church of God is equated with the "brotherhood," those with whom we consider ourselves to be in fellowship. It might even be determined by the one whom we would address as brother, or whom, should he visit, we would call upon to offer public prayer. This type of thinking is not new. Nearly a hundred years ago a correspondent wrote in the **American Christian Review:**

"I believe that the body of people known as the Church of Christ, the Christian Church, the Disciples of Christ, etc., is the true Church of God." [14]

To this writer the body of Christ was identical to the brotherhood as he viewed it.

Now, the church is indeed a brotherhood, but it is inevitable that our concept of the brotherhood will not precisely accord with that of Jesus. Should a group of truth seekers in another land agree to accept God's word as their sole spiritual guide and by this means obey from the heart that form of teaching revealed in it, would they not be just Christians? This very thing has happened on various occasions. But since we would know nothing of them, we would scarcely count them in our brotherhood. Even in our own land, are we so presumptuous as to conclude that only those we have chosen to list in our directories and count in our brotherhood are named in the Book of Life?

I have twice edited a directory of undenominational churches. Such directories have distinct value in assisting Christians in locating others of like faith. But they are at best imperfect, will include some that should be omitted, and will exclude others that ought to be included. They should never be considered the Lord's list of congregations whose candlesticks are before the throne of God.

The brotherhood concept is too exclusive. It does not just presume that "we" are **Christians only**, but supposes that "we" are the only Christians. Observe the comments of Joseph Franklin regarding the matter in the early Restoration Movement:

"The idea of denominationalism embraces the entire work of forming a party of professed Christians separate from all other professed Christians, and giving them a name which belongs to no others. It was held by the Reformers for many years that they were not doing this. They took the names, Christian and Disciples of Christ, but did not presume to appropriate them exclusively. Any other persons might use them as well. When they said they belonged to the Church of Christ they did not assume that other persons did not." [15]

It is often desirable that a group of churches in a given area work together to promote the cause of Christ. As such they constitute a fellowship, or brotherhood, if you prefer, but this relationship should never be viewed as one that excludes other individuals who have fully complied with the will of Christ in their acceptance of the gospel and the conduct of their lives.

How, then, shall we answer the question, "Are 'we' a denomination?" It is obvious that some in the restoration tradition have embraced the denominational viewpoint. This is true of the Disciples who not only acknowledge their sectarian status, but have a restructured organization that is avowedly denominational.

153

Other spiritual heirs of the Campbells and Stone possess many characteristics of denominationalism. Even though they may avoid sectarian terminology and denominational structure, they exhibit such a sectarian attitude that if they are not in fact denominational, they are seriously tainted by a denominational spirit.

It is also true that among the thousands of congregations in the Restoration Movement there are many shortcomings that may be pointed out. Some relate to issues discussed in this book. It is not hard to find unconsciously held sectarian attitudes. It is also possible to find doctrinal deviations from the New Testament pattern.

Nevertheless, many of these congregations are making an honest effort to restore New Testament Christianity, including the undenominational aspect. They recognize that restoration must be ongoing and they do not believe that they have arrived at a full realization of the truth in every particular. They not only call on men to forsake sectarianism, but they also emphasize the positive importance of being **Christians only.** There is a gap, of course, between theory and practice. They may not always recognize that this is true. But this is not really unusual. Is there not a practice gap in each of our lives between what we want to be and what we are, even as was true of Paul? (Romans 7:13-25). As we are imperfect beings, the practice of our faith is also imperfect. That one falls short in his love for his fellowmen or in his faith in Christ or in his dedication to the cause of the Master does not mean that he has ceased to be a Christian. Those churches that are striving to be undenominational do not usually come up to their standard and may even fall far short of the objective. But they are still trying, still working to that end. Therefore, they may justifiably speak of themselves as undenominational, while still acknowledging that they have not attained perfection.

I personally know of many congregations, that, with all of their shortcomings, are earnestly seeking to be truly biblical churches of Jesus Christ. I have no right to condemn them en masse because of the deficiencies I see in some.

Moreover, there are thousands of Christians who have risen above the spiritual conditions of the assemblies of which they are members. Like some in Sardis, they "have not soiled their garments" and they shall walk with Christ in white, "for they are worthy" (Revelation 3:4). They do not cry out like Elijah when he fled before Jezebel, "I only am left," but recognizing sectarianism in their midst, they seek to bring their fellow Christians to a fuller understanding of undenominational Christianity. They are, in fact, **JUST CHRISTIANS.**

## FOOTNOTES

1. Norman L. Parks, "Thy Ecclesia Come!", **Voices of Concern** (St. Louis: Mission Messenger, 1966), p. 84.

2. Ralph V. Graham, "Why I Left," **Voices of Concern,** p. 140.

3. Cecil May, Jr., "Undenominational Christianity," **Firm Foundation,** June 10, 1969.

4. **Directory of the Ministry of the Undenominational Fellowship of Christian Churches and Churches of Christ, 1973** (Springfield, Illinois: Directory of the Ministry, 1973), p. F-9.

5. See W. E. Garrison, **Religion Follows the Frontier** (New York and London: Harper and Brothers, 1931); Oliver Read Whitley, **Trumpet Call of Reformation** (St. Louis: Bethany Press, 1959); and David Edwin Harrell, Jr., **Quest for a Christian America** (Nashville, Tennessee: Disciples of Christ Historical Society, 1966), Vol. 1.

6. David Edwin Harrell, Jr., **Emergence of the 'Church of Christ' Denomination** (Lufkin, Texas: Gospel Guardian, no date), p. 20.

7. **Ibid.,** p. 24.

8. W. Carl Ketcherside, "Schisms and Parties," **Mission Messenger,** November, 1959, p. 8.

9. David Edwin Harrell, Jr., **Op. Cit.,** p. 31.

10. W. Carl Ketcherside, "What Divides Us?", **Mission Messenger,** August, 1959, p. 10.

11. Burnell S. Rawls, **Do I Belong to the Right Church?** (Corvallis, Oregon: Burnell Rawls, no date).

12. W. Carl Ketcherside, "Schisms and Parties," **Mission Messenger,** November, 1959, p. 4, 5.

13. George W. Butterfield, **The New Testament Church** (Delight, Arkansas: Gospel Light, 1949), p. 21.

14. A. Martin, "Reply to Joseph Franklin," **American Christian Review**, August 2, 1881, p. 245.

15. Joseph Franklin and J. A. Headington, **The Life and Times of Benjamin Franklin** (St. Louis: John Burns, 1879), pp. 319, 320.

# CHAPTER 12

# TRADITIONALISM

I vividly recall the worship of the rural congregation where my parents obeyed their Lord and where I frequently attended with them in my earliest years. Although we lived in town and worshipped there most of the time, we often spent summers in the country and worshipped at Summit. Frequently thereafter we would go back to visit. On at least one occasion I accompanied my father when he returned to preach in a series of meetings.

What stands out most clearly in my memory is that we always knelt for prayer. The folding wooden seats were hard on the arms when you leaned on them, especially if you thought the prayer was getting too long. One of the elders sat in a stiff armchair in the front and presided. Another member would start a song from his seat. Not infrequently it would be a sister. There was no designated song leader and never did the one directing stand before the assembly. The chairman would ask for exhortations and various brethren, standing at their seats, would edify the church from a selected passage of scripture. This was called mutual edification. (For most of its ninety year history Summit has had a "located" preacher only for short periods). When the Lord's supper was offered there were two silver plates for the bread and two silver cups. When the fruit of the vine was given, the presiding elder would first offer thanks, and then pour it into the cups from a tall silver decanter. Each member would then drink from one of the cups.

To many who have never "seen it done that way," this procedure may seem strange. Today few congregations kneel for prayer. For one thing, the pews are too close together. It may be hard to visualize a service without a regular preacher, and to think that the ordinary men in the church would be capable Sunday after Sunday of exhorting it as they did at Summit seems almost unthinkable. Summit was blessed with an unusual array of talent, and perhaps that is one reason the system worked. Many Christians have never partaken of the fruit of the vine except in individual cups (or glasses) and I suspect that some would think that the contagion of tuberculosis would be spread by the two chalices. And how could we possibly get along without a song leader waving his hand at us? Certainly in many places the idea of a sister starting the tune from her seat would produce a major controversy. I do not cite the way it was done at Summit to argue that this procedure was necessarily right in every respect, but to suggest how customs and practices vary from place to place.

Soon after I started working with a congregation in a large midwestern city a young man from another area moved to our community and began assembling with us. Following the morning worship he came to me with a concerned expression. "Brother Hawley," he inquired, "is it scriptural to have the Lord's supper before the sermon rather than after it?" He had never before seen the sacred feast observed in the early part of the worship period. When I assured him that God's word does not specify the precise order of worship he was satisfied and so far as I know was never again troubled about the matter. I have no reason to believe that he had been taught that partaking of the communion must follow the "sermon" since I later worked with his home congregation and never heard anyone there so affirm. His question was prompted, not by teaching, but by an unvarying practice which he came to equate with the law of God.

Most of us do not realize the extent to which customs fasten themselves on us. I recall the late Batsell Baxter relating that for a period a Texas congregation found it necessary to meet in the afternoon. A faithful sister immediately ceased worshipping with the saints. When queried as to the reason for her absence she responded that the church was meeting at an unscriptural hour, the scriptural hour, she explained, being 11:00 a.m. When asked, "Where does the Bible teach this?" she stammered a bit and then retorted, "Why, why, the Bible's all full of it!"

We may smile at such obvious misuse of scripture, if indeed this even constitutes a use. Yet we have all been influenced to some extent by customs and teachings which we, because everyone in our religious circle has accepted them, have unquestion-

158

ingly accepted as divine writ. Many of these practices are indeed biblical, but there is always danger in presuming that because the way we do it is scriptural all other ways are wrong. This is traditionalism, one of the greatest hindrances to the cause of undenominational Christianity. For if our customs are equated with law, we are teaching an adulterated gospel and asking the world to accept a plea which we deny in practice.

The Greek word **paradosis,** translated **tradition** a dozen times in the New Testament, literally means "a giving over." The tradition might be transmitted from generation to generation "either by word of mouth or by letter" (2 Thessalonians 2:15). While we usually think of traditions as being passed on orally, the word is also employed in the New Testament to apply to those things conveyed by writing. The Pharisees of the first century had many of these religious customs, related to such things as ceremonial washings, the fringes of one's garments, and how far one could travel on the sabbath day. Jesus condemned the Pharisees, not because of their traditons, but because they used them to nullify God's word. He declared, "You have a fine way of rejecting the commandment of God, in order to keep your tradition! For Moses said, 'Honor your father and your mother'; and, 'He who speaks evil of father or mother, let him surely die'; but you say, 'If a man tells his father or his mother, What you would have gained from me is Corban' (that is, given to God)—then you no longer permit him to do anything for his father or mother, thus making void the word of God through your tradition which you hand on. And many such things you do" (Mark 7:9-13). Traditions are not wrong simply because they are traditions, but they may become wrong when improperly used.

Paul enjoins the Thessalonians to adhere to the divine traditions given to them. "So then, brethren, stand firm and hold to the traditions which you were taught by us, either by word of mouth or by letter" (2 Thessalonians 2:15). Here he refers to the apostolic message, those precepts revealed by the Holy Spirit, and conveyed to them both in apostolic writing and the spoken word. The New Testament preserves these traditions, and were the apostles to return to earth today, they would deliver these same traditions by word of mouth. Of course, their message would be the same as the written traditions of the New Testament.

These divine traditions, however, are quite different from the human traditions of the Pharisees of Jesus' day or of the Catholic Church or of ours. While some of the Catholic traditions are probably accurate, there is no positive way of authenticating them if they are not substantiated by the written word of God. Unless one is willing to acknowledge that the Catholic Church has infallibly preserved these traditions, they can no more be unreservedly accepted than the tradition that George Washington cut down his father's cherry tree!

Every society has its cultural patterns and traditions. Jesus was born into a Jewish religious world influenced by the Sadducees and Pharisees which was in turn affected in its outlook by the Roman world of government and the Greek world of culture and education. The New Testament abounds in references to these influences and neither the teachings of Jesus nor the history of the apostolic church can be separated from the background against which they were set. It is said of Jesus, "And when he was twelve years old, they went up (to the Passover) according to **custom**" (Luke 2:42). When he ate the last supper with the twelve they doubtless reclined at the table according to Jewish convention rather than sitting in straight chairs as would we. When he died, "They took the body of Jesus, and bound it in linen clothes with spices, as is the burial custom of the Jews" (John 19:40). The Judaizing party in the early church taught, "Unless you are circumcised according to the **custom** of Moses, you cannot be saved" (Acts 15:1). Paul and Silas were dragged before the rulers in the market place of Philippi with the charge, "These men are Jews and they are disturbing our city. They advocate **customs** which it is not lawful for us Romans to accept or practice" (Acts 16:20, 21).

As Wendell Broom suggests, Jesus took various attitudes toward the different cultural practices he encountered. Some, such as the Jewish practices of prayer and study, he **commanded**. He apparently **adapted** to his own use the Essene practice of water baptism and commanded it as essential to entrance into his kingdom. The Lord's supper is at least partially an adaptation of the Jewish passover. On the other hand, Jesus **opposed** Roman idolatry and emperor worship and took issue with the overly permissive attitude of the Jews toward divorce. Jesus **diverted** some practices and turned them to his own purposes. For example, "Gehenna" or the Valley of Hinnom was the city dump that constantly burned in the valley south of Jerusalem. It had been defiled many years earlier when kings Ahaz and Manasseh burned their sons there as offerings in idol worship (2 Chronicles 28:3, 33:6). But Jesus used the word, translated for us as **hell,** to describe the place of eternal fire. There were other customs to which Jesus **conformed** such as feet washing, kissing by way of greeting, and the dress of first century Galilee and Judea. He accepted these because they were part of the culture of the

160

people. And then there were those customs which Jesus and the apostles **utilized** for their own purposes. They taught in the Jewish synagogue because this convenience was a means of spreading the word. Paul had Timothy circumcised in order to avert unnecessary Jewish criticism. When he saw an opportunity to engage the Athenian philosophers in religious discussion, he gladly went with them to the Areopagus, the place provided for such debates. [1]

The good news of Jesus is a universal message existing without regard to time or culture. In the fullness of God's time it was first given to the Jewish people of the first century. It was garbed in the trappings of that civilization. But strip away those externals and you discover a message with meaning for every society in every century. The problem facing the early church was the pressure of society seeking to force upon it cultural practices alien to the basic story of the gospel. Thus it was necessary for the apostles to oppose Judaistic tendencies that would make Christianity subservient to the law of Moses. They condemned the fleshly lust of Corinthian culture that would corrupt its morals. They fought the speculations of gnosticism that would distort the true nature of Christ. All of these were external forces seeking to pollute the stream of pure Christianity emanating from Jesus and the apostles he commissioned. Neither Jesus nor those he sent forth opposed the practices of society just for the joy of being different. Our Lord cast the money-changers out of the temple because their business dealings were corrupting the house of God, not because he sought to overturn the establishment. In his daily activities he conformed to the customs of the average Jew of his time. But he stood foursquare against the perversions of God's moral and religious laws. When the essence of the message of the new covenant was threatened, his apostles likewise took an uncompromising stand against every contaminating influence.

In the post-apostolic period the culture of society began to adversely intrude itself upon the church. The simple congregational structure of the apostolic body was replaced by a pyramidal type of organization patterned after the Roman government. Soon there were bishops, archbishops, metropolitans, and even a pope, all having their counterpart in the Roman system. The pagan festival of the winter solstice was changed in purpose to celebrate the birth of Jesus and became known as the mass of Christ or Christmas. Celebration of the resurrection of Christ was mixed with the Norse festival called Ostara or Eostre. Today we know it as Easter. Likewise, the medieval robes of another age have survived in the clerical dress of Catholics and some Protestants.

Every religious society has been influenced by those who led the way. A good example is seen in the Amish and Mennonites:

"The German language, the European dress, the farming methods that were popular in the days of the strength of their movement, became so enraptured and hallowed in their eyes that those customs have survived in their practice even down to this present day. In Delaware and Pennsylvania, you see men and women who still read their German Bibles, the language that was used when their reformation began—the hallowed language. You see them still wearing the same kind of dress, still driving horses—no automobiles, no telephones, no moving pictures of any kind."[2]

The Baptists, Methodists, Presbyterians, Episcopalians are all debtors in philosophies and observances to their spiritual ancestors. Too often the insights of a Luther or Calvin or Wesley that have produced a reformation pointing to Christ have become submerged in a morass of tradition with the original struggle for simple Christianity being drowned in a sea of denominationalism. Thus, "crystallization of custom has been the germinating power of sectarianism."[3] Usually those enmeshed in traditionalism are unable to distinguish between their traditions and the precepts of God's eternal word. Perhaps the Amish would defend their buggies as divinely authorized in contrast to the automobile. The Lutheran accepts the concept that the infant is capable of belief, not because it is taught in scripture, but because Luther put it in his catechism over four hundred years ago.[4]

It is not too difficult to see how previous generations have influenced their spiritual descendants if we are talking about others and not ourselves. It is, indeed, difficult as Robert Burns observed, "to see oursels as ithers see us!" But, in fact, we are all affected by the ideas of those who have gone before us. Who can say that he has not been touched in some way by Luther's views on faith or John Wesley's on holiness? Have we not sung Luther's "A Mighty Fortress Is Our God" and "Jesus Lover of My Soul" written by Wesley's brother, Charles? If we sing these hymns, do we not acknowledge the truthfulness of the words?

The Reformation of the Nineteenth Century has also stamped its culture upon those who have embraced the basic principles enunciated by the Campbells and Stone. True, the term "Campbellite" has been properly rejected as unworthy of those seeking to be just Christians, although we may wonder what would have been the reaction had Alexander Campbell looked upon the name with favor rather than with disdain. Yet, how many practices and teachings have been inherited from those great teachers of the last century? When I was younger we conducted "protracted meetings" once or twice a year. Today they are more often called "gospel meetings." It never occurred to me to inquire where the word "protracted" came from until I ran across a statement in the biography of Benjamin Franklin, the gospel preacher, which explained the origin:

"The ordinary monthly visit at the first, as now, comprehended a meeting on Saturday night and two on Sunday. For these regular visits preachers did not always, at the first, receive a stipulated amount; but, where it was promised, the price ranged from seventy-five to one hundred dollars per annum. If occasion seemed to call for it, the preacher was expected, for the same amount, to stay and 'protract' the meetings for a week."[5]

There it is! A protracted meeting, originally, was an extension of a regular monthly preaching appointment. Through the years the term survived but its original meaning was lost.

It is customary among American churches rooted historically in the Restoration Movement to sing a song of invitation at the conclusion of the service to give sinners an opportunity to respond in obedience to the gospel. So universal has the practice become that some have concluded that the only way one can indicate his intent to be baptized is "to walk down the aisle." It is doubtful that this was a practice in the early church. Its origin is traced to the revivalism of the early nineteenth century in which mourners seeking a religious experience were invited to the front of the assembly to pray at the "anxious seat" for conversion. In the early history of the Stone movement, this played an important part. On one occasion in 1807 or 1808 Stone himself called on the mourners to repent and be baptized for remission of sins. He later recounted that his appeal had a chilling effect, and he did not again for a number of years invite people to respond for this purpose.

The first person baptized as a result of an invitation extended specifically for that reason seems to have been Tolbert Fanning. B. F. Hall, a New Light preacher, was preaching in Lauderdale County, Alabama, in 1826. He had been struck by the inability of some to be comforted at the mourner's bench, and therefore offered an invitation to be immersed for the remission of sins. Fanning responded. A little over a year later, Walter Scott, a Campbell associate, began the same practice in his evangelistic efforts in the Western Reserve with astounding results.[6]

The invitation hymn, therefore, grew out of the revivalism of the last century as the custom of calling men to the "altar" to pray was modified in the Stone movement by inviting them instead to be baptized. Originally an evangelistic tool, it became standard at all worship periods among many churches in the Restoration Movement. It is not the purpose here to question the right to sing an invitation song, but rather to point out that it is a custom that must be justified only on grounds of expediency. If congregations continue to use this method, as most will probably do, they should recognize that it is a custom and that others should not be criticized as having departed from the faith should they decide to discontinue its use.

Each congregation has its distinctive customs. Most churches assemble on Sunday mornings for Bible classes lasting one hour followed by a worship period of similar duration. Usually there will also be an evening assembly. Prayer meeting or midweek Bible study falls on Wednesday night except in a few cases where it is on Thursday. In some places it would be unthinkable to propose a schedule change. Why not have Sunday Bible classes after the worship period? Or suppose that the church always had a potluck dinner following its morning service after which the congregation would again assemble to praise God, thus doing away with the evening worship? The time spent together would be greater, but the omission of the evening period might cause some objections because established tradition was being changed.

In many congregations the way the worship is conducted never varies. The idea that this is **the** right way may result. Occasionally a church will consciously change its order of worship to combat the problem only to settle into a new procedure which is never altered. Naturally, visiting friends have questions about the way things are done so explanations are in order. To avoid confusion when the contribution is taken up immediately after the communion is offered, the one presiding may announce, "Separate and apart from the Lord's supper, we now take up a collection." Soon the explanation becomes a part of the tradition, even if the Lord's supper and the contribution are separated in time during the worship.

The church building itself has become part of tradition. The early Christians did not own houses of worship. A rented hall or a home probably served in most cases as the place of assembly. But the religious world has long been wedded to the church building and those in the Restoration Movement have gone along with the pattern. Since the building has become a symbol of permanency for religious groups and rented facilities would often be difficult to secure, it is probably wise that this expedient be observed. However, there can be little doubt that the custom has caused some Christians to be so attached to the edifice that they are unable to conceive of the church functioning without it. Too often the building has become the place where one discharges his Christian reponsibilities. After a couple of hours on Sunday morning in Bible study and worship, he goes home unconsciously feeling that he has done his duty until the next Lord's day arrives. For him the building is Christianity. Should the building burn and a temporary hall be used for an afternoon worship period, he might find himself unable to function properly as a Christian because the symbol of his Christianity has been destroyed.

The process by which customs crystalize into traditions is succinctly stated by Wendell Broom as follows:

1. A necessary choice.

2. A wise expedient.

3. A unanimous agreement.

4. A constant usage.

5. A time-honored custom.

6. An unquestioned acceptance.

7. A sacred ordinance.

8. An infallible and unalterable decree. [7]

Broom then proceeds to analyze these eight steps in this way:

"NUMBER ONE—the necessary choice: We've got to make choices—that's inevitable. NUMBER TWO—the wise expedient: Our choices have to be wise choices—that's essential. NUMBER THREE—the unanimous agreement: Wait now—it doesn't have to be unanimous. We can agree on a wise expedient and most of us can agree with it, but let's remind ourselves, brethren, that there are other judgments possible, and their alternatives may be as wise as ours. Human judgment is liable to error, and since we are the ones choosing, let's remember that this is not God's decree, it's our judgment, and there can be differences. NUMBER FOUR—the constant usage: Vary it occasionally. One time

165

in our congregation we had a class studying the Lord's supper. There were some children in that class, who in reply to the question, 'What is the Lord's supper?' answered very quickly, 'The bread and the wine and the collection.' Why did they answer so? Because of constant usage. The next Sunday, we had the collection at the beginning of the service and the Lord's supper at the end, and it worked. They understand it now. Vary the usage, and break it up. Two songs and a prayer and a song and a sermon. Break it up. If you don't, you're going to have a generation of children that think that's the only way it can possibly be done. NUMBER FIVE—the time-honored custom: Now here comes in emotion. Brethren, you can handle that one best by gentle questions and suggestions. Usually mother and dad enter into this one. 'That's the way my mother and father did it, and you say it's not right???' Brethren, that's why the word 'gentle' must come in here. You'd better do it gently, and you'd better tread carefully, because this is emotion. NUMBER SIX— the unquestioned acceptance: If 'mother and dad did it that way because grandmother and granddad did it that way,' then you've really got an emotional charge back of it. Any alternative that you propose must be a loving alternative, and a loving proposal. You go in rough shod and you're going to get a rough response. But you put in a loving proposal about this thing which has become unquestioned and you're going to have better results. NUMBER SEVEN—the 'sacred ordinance': When a chosen expedient has been so widely used for so long that people begin to think that's the way God commanded it, then how are we going to prevent it crystallizing? There must be a reverent request for investigation. This is what the apostle Paul did and he had the right to do it differently. He went to Antioch and the Judaizers were saying, 'You Gentiles have to be circumcised or you can't go to heaven.' Paul had the right to jump in with both feet and say, 'It's not so, and I'm an apostle of Christ and I can give you a revelation of God to prove it's not so.' He could have done it that way, but he didn't. Do you know what he did? He made a reverent request for investigation: 'Brethren, let's go down to Jerusalem and let's talk this thing over with the apostles down there. Let's see what they say about it. Let's find out what God wants us to do here.' And despite all the emotion that was piled up behind the Jewish mind on the subject, Paul reverently investigated it with them. He knew the answer, surely, but he did it so that he might win his brethren who weren't so far advanced in the knowledge of Christ as he was.

"Then, NUMBER EIGHT—when people think our expedient choice is an infallible and unalterable decree: What's to be done then? This custom has grown so deeply rooted that everyone thinks it is God speaking and that it isn't just a custom. What's to be done then? Paul faced that problem and I think he faced it best in the book of Galatians. He took an opposition to it. It was strong. His opposition was godly, yes, it was a holy opposition, but brethren, it was an unshaking opposition. Read him in Galatians to see that dogged determination to oppose the Judaizers." [8]

Traditionalism in practice is not the only way Christians are affected by those who preceded them. Interpretation of scripture often reflects the conclusions of an earlier generation which may never have been carefully reexamined in the light of God's word. The writer has often heard John 9:31 cited as evidence that God will not hear the prayer of the alien sinner. The passage reads, "We know that God heareth not sinners." What those quoting fail to point out is that the statement was made by an uninspired blind man talking about miracles and not prayers, and so it does not have authority as though an apostle were speaking. In examining the subject, faithfulness to God's word also requires a study of the Lord's statement: "Cornelius, your prayer has been heard and your alms have been remembered before God" (Acts 10:31). While the original source of the above argument is uncertain, we may be sure that one generation has heard it from another and that those who have quoted it without explaining the identity of the speaker have not critically examined the passage for themselves.

The frequently cited five steps to be saved—hearing, believing, repenting, confessing, and being baptized—are but a modification of the five finger exercise first used by Walter Scott in the Western Reserve—faith, repentance, baptism, remission of sins, gift of the Holy Spirit. [9]

Some arguments used today by proclaimers of the word may be traced back to Alexander Campbell. For example, a popular series of filmstrips uses the line of reasoning that there are four things necessary to constitute a physical kingdom—a king, a territory, subjects, and a law. The same principle applies in the spiritual kingdom of Christ. [10] But in 1835 Alexander Campbell wrote:

"We must understand the type, or we can not understand the anti-type. We must understand that which is natural before we can understand that which is spiritual. What then are the essential elements of a kingdom as existing among men? They are five, viz.: King, Constitution, Subjects, Laws, and Territory." [11]

Campbell then showed that these elements are in the divine kingdom. With a single omission (constitution), the argument advanced in the filmstrip is the same as that of Campbell. It is valid reasoning and is well applied in the filmstrip. It should not be discarded simply because Campbell used it. But we should recognize that we are deeply indebted to scholars of former years for many of our concepts. Was the argument even originally Campbell's or did he borrow it from one who preceded him?

It is also possible to reject practices as unbiblical when in fact the reason for opposition is essentially traditional. In the last century when the dispute over instrumental music was at its height in the Restoration Movement, a companion question was that of the legitimacy of the choir. The two were linked in argument and those favoring the instrument usually accepted the choir while those opposing the instrument in worship rejected not only the choir, but all non-congregational singing. Today there are few congregations among those churches not using the instrument that would consider having any kind of special singing such as solos or quartets. However, 1 Corinthians 14:26 establishes that the singing of solos for the purpose of edification was used in the apostolic church. That the context of the passage relates to spiritual gifts and that "special numbers" can be abused by the singers in seeking to demonstrate their abilities does not alter the basic principle. Yet it is safe to say that in many places today were the preacher to edify the church by song rather than the spoken word he would be accused of violating the teaching of scripture requiring only congregational singing!

What should be our attitude toward custom and tradition? First, customs are not necessarily wrong and should not be changed just for the sake of doing things differently. What is important is that customs be recognized for what they are—expedients of men rather than holy writ.

Second, each practice, and each interpretation, should be reexamined carefully in the light of scripture to determine what is traditional and what is actually revealed in the Bible. Erroneous ideas must be rejected, even if hallowed by years of usage. It is important that we seek to restore New Testament Christianity, not the Restoration Movement.

Third, we must make our message relate to today, not yesterday. The evangelistic meeting was effective in the last century. Does it still fulfill a need today, or are there better ways of accomplishing the same end? Are midweek Bible classes conducted at the church building still the best way of providing additional instruction during the week, or could this more effectively be done by a series of home Bible studies on different nights of the week? It has been suggested that the 11:00 a.m. Sunday worship hour was chosen years ago because it was half way between the farmer's milkings. Since most people no longer milk cows, would it be better to meet another time of day?

Fourth, count the cost before making changes in the customary. Some things are permissible which are not expedient. If the church is torn apart in dissension over matters of expediency, is a change really worth it in view of the inevitable heartache and the souls placed in jeopardy? "Do not for the sake of food, destroy the work of God" (Romans 14:20).

Fifth, we must patiently teach the oracles of God, stripping away as best we can the vestiges of traditionalism which color our practices and interpretations. Traditions result from years of practice and cannot be removed overnight. Patient teaching in the spirit of love will produce more good than a campaign to overturn the establishment.

Let us remember that traditionalism is a contaminant of undenominational Christianity. To be effectively conveyed to the world that message must be unencumbered by the barnacles of tradition that have fastened themselves upon the body of Christ and hinder the spread of the good news of Jesus.

## FOOTNOTES

1. Wendell Broom, Sr., **The Crystallization of Custom** (Abilene, Texas: Abilene Christian College, no date), pp. 2, 3.

2. **Ibid.**, pp. 5, 6.

3. **Ibid.**, p. 6.

4. C. Gausewitz, editor, **Doctor Martin Luther's Small Catechism** (Milwaukee: Northwestern Publishing, 1942), p. 143.

5. Joseph Franklin and J. A. Headington, **The Life and Times of Benjamin Franklin** (St. Louis: John Burns, 1879), p. 72.

6. Thomas H. Olbricht, "The Invitation: A Historical Survey," **Restoration Quarterly**, Vol. 5, No. 1, 1961, pp. 12 - 14.

7. Wendell Broom, Sr., **Op. Cit.**, p. 15.

8. **Ibid.**, pp. 15 - 17.

9. William Baxter, **Life of Elder Walter Scott** (Nashville, Tennessee: Gospel Advocate, no date), p. 184.

10. Jule Miller, **The Visualized Bible Study Series, Number Three, The Christian Age** (Houston, Texas: Gospel Services, 1961), p. 7.

11. Alexander Campbell, **The Christian System** (Cincinnati: Standard Publishing), p. 125.

# CHAPTER 13

# THE FELLOWSHIP
# OF THE SAVED

It was in 1827 that an evangelistic fire swept Ohio's Western Reserve. Fanning its flames was Walter Scott, the most eloquent preacher of the early Restoration Movement. Under his teaching thousands heard the word of God and hundreds of them obeyed it. Skeptics came to discover the error in the message of this proclaimer of good news but went away convinced that they had found the truth. Such a man was Aylette Raines, a thirty-year-old "Restorationist" preacher whose beliefs included the opinion that the wicked would eventually be blessed. After hearing Scott preach, Raines sought out fellow universalist Ebenezer Williams to see if he could refute Scott's views. For four days they conferred after which they immersed one another into Jesus and determined to cast their lot with the fledgling effort to restore New Testament Christianity.[1]

The conversion of Raines posed the first serious threat to the harmony of the Campbell movement. Here was a gifted man who could be an effective instrument in the conversion of many. But, by his own admission, he still held universalist ideas relating to the ultimate salvation of all mankind. This doctrine was not only unbiblical, but in the minds of some endangered the proclamation of their message. Should he be accepted into their fellowship or rejected as a heretic because of his personal opinions?[2] We will shortly examine the way this question was answered by a principle which was fundamental to the teaching of fellowship in the Restoration Movement.

No aspect of undenominational Christianity is more difficult to

171

clarify than fellowship. This is not because of ambiguity of the biblical teachings on the subject, but because of the practical problems posed when we attempt to apply these principles.

Any examination of fellowship in the New Testament must focus on the meaning of the Greek word **koinonia** and its related terms. Our English versions variously translate it as **fellowship, communication, communion, distribution, contribution, partnership, participation, sharing,** etc. The basic idea of the word is that of sharing in common. When applied to relationships among Christians it suggests those views, thoughts, and actions in which they are one.

Fundamental to our fellowship with one another is that we enjoy with God. John declares that "our fellowship is with the Father and with his Son Jesus Christ" (1 John 1:3). It is through the graciousness of the Father that we have partnership with the Son. "God is faithful, by whom you were called into the fellowship of his Son, Jesus Christ our Lord" (1 Corinthians 1:9). The communion we share with God is a vertical relationship between the great and the small, the Creator and the created.

The horizontal relationship of Christians with one another proceeds from the vertical. It is horizontal because it links those equal in the sight of the Father. In the human family brothers and sisters enjoy kinship because they have common parents. That our mutual relationship stems from that we have with Christ is stressed by John, "Every one who loves the parent loves the child" (1 John 5:1). Another passage possibly bearing on this idea is 1 John 1:6, 7. "If we say that we have fellowship with him while we walk in darkness, we lie and do not live according to the truth; but if we walk in the light, as he is in the light, we have fellowship with one another, and the blood of Jesus his Son cleanses us from all sin." It is disputable whether the phrase "fellowship with one another" refers to the association among Christians or the relationship of the child of God with the Father. Regardless, our fellowship with one another does rest on each person's communion with God attained by walking in the light of our Lord. When we cease to be in spiritual step with Christ, we also cease to harmonize with one another.

Fellowship among disciples of Christ is found in many areas of our lives. It begins with acceptance of a common doctrine. When John wrote about fellowship in his first epistle he was discussing the apostles' doctrine about Christ (1 John 1:1-3). Paul rests his condemnation of an unequal yoking of believers with unbelievers on a lack of common agreement in fundamental faith (2 Corinthians 6:14-18). Through the centuries doctrinal disagreement has been one of the chief causes of disruption of Christian fellowship. When men cannot agree upon the content of the gospel message it is difficult for them to walk together.

The sharing of religious ideology produces joint participation in many areas of life. Thus the early Christians prayed together (Acts 12:5, 12), opened their homes to one another (Acts 21:8-10). shared their meals (1 Corinthians 5:11; Jude 12), enjoyed mutual company (Romans 15:24), encouraged one another (Hebrews 10:23-25), and met jointly in worship on the first day of the week to partake of the Lord's supper (Acts 20:7; 1 Corinthians 11:20).

Among the Jerusalem disciples this common faith resulted in a sharing of material goods. "And all who believed were together and had all things in common; and they sold their possessions and goods and distributed them to all, as any had need" (Acts 2:44, 45). While the complete sharing here mentioned is not indicated elsewhere in the New Testament, there are other instances of pooling of goods to meet a need. The disciples in Antioch contributed to the welfare of the Judean disciples in time of famine (Acts 11:27-30), and Paul later took up a collection from the Gentile Christians to alleviate the material needs of disciples in Jerusalem (Romans 15:26, 27). He specifically desig- nated this action as fellowship in declaring that the Macedonian disciples had besought "us with much entreaty in regard of this grace and the fellowship in the ministering to the saints" (2 Corinthians 8:4—A.S.V.).

Fellowship in Christ extends to the work we share in Him. James, Peter, and John gave to Paul and Barnabas "the right hand of fellowship" by way of endorsing their labors among the Gentiles (Galatians 2:9). The saints in Philippi so participated in Paul's work of proclamation by contributing to his financial needs that he wrote them that he was thankful for their "partnership in the gospel from the first day until now" (Philip- pians 1:5). As we jointly work to spread the good news of the kingdom of Christ, we enjoy true fellowship in Christ.

This brief sketch of fellowship among followers of Jesus in apostolic times reveals a broader picture of Christian relation- ship than generally thought of today. To some people fellowship primarily implies association in eating a meal in a "fellowship hall." While it is clear that early Christians did eat together (Jude 12), the sharing of a meal being an aspect of fellowship, such a definition does not begin to comprehend the totality of the New Testament viewpoint. Others conceive of fellowship largely in terms of worship. Thus a disciple who sings and prays and shares the Lord's supper with his fellow Christians for an hour on Sunday morning is said to be "in fellowship," even though he may not associate with them again for another week. He may even shun their company on most occasions, but because his name is on the "church roll" he is declared to be "in full fellowship" while in fact the area of life he shares with other saints is very limited. What is really meant by fellowship is not so much **sharing** as **recognition.** In the contemporary sense when men speak of being in fellowship they imply that they recognize others as Christians and as enjoying a proper relationship with God. This falls far short of the New Testament idea, although it is true that recognition precedes our intimate sharing in Christ. Furthermore, to acknowledge one as a brother is not necessarily the same as enjoying fellowship with him. If two people cannot work and worship together because of basic differences, there may be recognition without real fellowship.

It is also apparent that in the biblical sense there are different areas of fellowship. The Christian who gathers with other disciples around the Lord's table, but does not give financially to spread the Word, has fellowship in one area but not in another. Those who enjoy only the communion of worship are not participating with other children of God in the same measure as those who also enjoy a social relationship and who mutually teach lost souls. Failure to establish a joint relationship in one area does not preclude the possibility of such a relationship in another. However, if the inability to participate jointly in one respect results from basic ideological differences, practically speaking the possibility of fellowship in other respects is compromised and may become impossible. It is precisely at this point that undenominational Christians encounter their major difficulties. If theological differences separate us in one area, can true fellowship in the biblical sense be possible?

Any discussion of fellowship assumes that there is a family within which spiritual kinship may be found. Peter admonishes us to "love the brotherhood" (1 Peter 2:17). The New Testament abounds in passages using "brother" and "sister" in the spiritual sense. When Jesus was informed that his mother and brothers were asking for him, he responded, "Whoever does the will of God is my brother, and sister, and mother" (Mark 3:35). Thus spiritual relationship in Christ is determined by doing God's will. All of this implies that there is a process by which one becomes a member of the divine family. One writer explains it in this way:

"Every person on this earth, motivated by faith in Jesus as the

Messiah, the Son of God, who has turned away from sin, and submitted to immersion of his body in water on the basis of that belief, is a member of God's family, and is my brother." [3]

While some will disagree about the degree of understanding required by the Lord when one is immersed, all should be able to acknowledge that if one has obeyed the gospel in the biblical sense and has been born into the family of God, he is a Christian brother. Our discussion of fellowship in this chapter pertains to those who are actually children of God, and does not relate to those professed Christians who in fact have not obeyed the good news of Jesus.

The scriptures teach that there are times when Christians are to withdraw their fellowship from a brother. Paul instructed the Corinthians how to deal with sins of immorality. "I wrote to you in my letter not to associate with immoral men; not at all meaning the immoral of this world, or the greedy and robbers, or idolaters, since then you would need to go out of the world. But rather I wrote to you not to associate with any one who bears the name of brother if he is guilty of immorality or greed, or is an idolater, reviler, drunkard, or robber—not even to eat with such a one" (1 Corinthians 5:9-11). In considering the contentious brother, Paul counseled Titus, "As for a man who is factious, after admonishing him once or twice, have nothing more to do with him, knowing that such a person is perverted and sinful; he is self-condemned" (Titus 3:10, 11). Again, "I appeal to you brethren, to take note of those who create dissensions and difficulties, in opposition to the doctrine which you have been taught; avoid them" (Romans 16:17). In the letters to the seven churches of Asia Jesus through John admonished the disciples in those congregations to reject false teachers (Revelation 2, 3). Paul warned Timothy against Hymenaeus and Philetus "who have swerved from the truth by holding that the resurrection is past already" (2 Timothy 2:18). Quite obviously, therefore, there are some brethren who should not be extended the fellowship of other Christians. However, it is seldom easy to decide from whom we should withdraw. The problem is especially difficult when matters of doctrinal truth and error are at stake rather than the immoral or factious conduct of a Christian.

We return to the story of Aylette Raines and his request for acceptance into the early Restoration Movement. The issue of his recognition (for this is what is implied both then and now in fellowship) was raised at the annual meeting of the Mahoning Association in 1828. While this was two years before the body officially dissolved, it had by then lost many of its denominational

175

characteristics. Hayden describes the 1828 gathering in this way:

"The association came together purely and simply as an assembly of Christians. Though under the forms and name of a Baptist association, the creed system was abandoned, and neither that denominational name, nor any other, was on its standards. Men of nearly all the religious bodies, many of them leaders therein, leaving the technics of the party, but retaining their faith, hope, and love, mingled together as disciples of the common Lord; now in the one body, possessing the one spirit, rejoicing in the same hope, submitting themselves to the same Lord, through the one faith and the one baptism, they worshiped together the same God and Father of all Christian people. This great occasion was a grand demonstration of the possibility of the union of Christians on original Bible ground. It was no longer a theory. It was then an actual, accomplished fact." [4]

The introductory message was delivered by Alexander Campbell who selected Romans 14:1 as his text: "As for the man who is weak in faith, welcome him, but not for disputes over opinions." Campbell classified all subjects relating to the Christian religion under three heads: (1) matters of personal knowledge; (2) things of faith; (3) matters of opinion. After showing that all of us know some things as a result of personal experience, he pointed out that faith rests on testimony and then quoted Romans 10:17, "So faith comes from what is heard, and what is heard comes by the preaching of Christ." He associated faith with the fundamental facts of the gospel and concluded that upon these things Christians cannot be divided.

On this third point Campbell established that it is in the realm of opinion, including creedal statements, that disciples of Christ divide. He asserted that, based on the principle laid down by Paul in Romans 14:1, we ought to receive one another, that is, we ought to accept without reservation those Christians who differ from us in matters of opinion.

When his case was brought before the assembly, Raines declared that while he still entertained Restorationist sentiments relating to the salvation of the wicked, he regarded them as opinions, would not preach them nor contend for them, but would confine himself to the simple gospel message. The matter was put to the assembly and based on the principle laid down by Campbell, Raines was accepted in spite of his heretical views. [5]

Raines' personal observation on this approach is instructive:

176

"I was dealt with, and my case managed, by Bro. Campbell and all the chief brethren in very great kindness and wisdom. Had they attempted to brow-beat me I might have been ruined forever. But treating me kindly, at the same time that they convinced me that my opinion, whether true or false, dwindled into nothingness in comparison with the faith of the gospel, redeemed me. I became a day and night preacher of the gospel, and my mind becoming absorbed in this vast work, the opinion faded, and in ten months was numbered with all my former errors." [6]

Alexander Campbell's position was essentially the same as that taken earlier by his father in the **Declaration and Address.** This document can be analyzed on the basis of one of the fundamental mottoes of the Restoration Movement. The original statement, "Unity in essentials, liberty in non-essentials, charity in all things," is ascribed to Rupertus Meldenius. Thomas Campbell modified it to read, "In faith unity; in opinions liberty; in all things charity." The **Declaration and Address** clearly distinguished between faith and opinion in calling for a return to the original form of Christianity

" . . . without attempting to inculcate anything of human authority, of private opinion, or inventions of men, as having any place in the constitution, faith, or worship, of the Christian Church, or anything as matter of Christian faith or duty, for which there can not be expressly produced a 'Thus saith the Lord, either in express terms, or by approved precedent.'" [7]

Campbell's motto delimits the range in which Christian unity is to be sought. There is a core of Christian teaching which is fundamental to fellowship. Unless there can be agreement upon these matters, there cannot be a unity acceptable to Christ.

On the other hand, there is a broad spectrum of things properly classified as opinions. Paul's warning that the weak in the faith should not be rejected on the basis of opinion was illustrated by the apostle. "One man believes he may eat anything, while the weak man eats only vegetables. Let not him who eats despise him who abstains, and let not him who abstains pass judgment on him who eats; for God has welcomed him. Who are you to pass judgment on the servant of another? It is before his own master that he stands or falls. And he will be upheld, for the Master is able to make him stand. One man esteems one day as better than another, while another man esteems all days alike. Let every one be fully convinced in his own mind" (Romans 14:2-5). Specifically Paul was declaring that whether one does or

177

does not eat meat, or whether he does or does not observe certain days in a religious sense ought not to be ground for severing fellowship. These are matters of opinion, and although we should not conclude that there is not a right and wrong position on each, they are not part of that body of truth called **faith** upon which there must be agreement for brotherhood to exist.

It ought to be added that Paul was considering private opinions and was not stating that it is acceptable for one to try to force his views of eating meats or observing days on another. What is contemplated is the believing of an opinion, not its active promotion.

The emphasis in the motto on love—"in all things charity"— is an element frequently overlooked in the Restoration Movement. One does not have to be contentious to "contend for the faith." Too often separation has resulted, not so much from doctrinal differences, as from personality clashes and a failure to exhibit the spirit of Christian love. Many, many of our difficulties can be overcome if we will but restore this aspect of the Christian faith.

Because of its brevity, the slogan we are considering falls short in one important area. While correctly distinguishing between faith and opinion, it provides no method by which to determine what are matters of faith. This must be ascertained by biblical interpretation. While all ought to be able to recognize the distinct areas of faith and opinion, no two people will agree completely as to what constitutes either. One man's faith is another man's opinion. The one who places a teaching in the category of faith will insist upon agreement on it as a condition of fellowship, while the one who assigns it to opinion will doubtless feel that his Christian liberty has been abridged when the other insists on conformity. Nevertheless, the relationship between faith, opinion, and love is both valid and vital in our quest for unity in Christ.

Sometimes it helps in analyzing our problems to inquire how they came about. A backward glance at the rupture of fellowship in the Restoration Movement should assist in our search for a solution to present day conditions.

Several initial observations should be made about conditions prior to the division over societies, instrumental music, and related matters. As previously noted, the Restoration Movement emphasized the twin objectives of Christian union and the restoration of apostolic Christianity. Any effort which tried so hard to promote religious unity would not quickly divide and in so doing defeat one of its major goals. Except for the defection of Dr. John Thomas and the Christadelphians in the 1840's, there was no serious breach in the Reformation of the Nineteenth Century until the 1880's. Numerically speaking even the Thomas departure was minor.

Furthermore, the restoration leaders were virtually unanimous in their desire to avoid a break in fellowship. One of the staunchest opponents of the American Christian Missionary Society was Tolbert Fanning, yet Fanning declared in 1859 before the annual meeting of that body:

"But I am happy to say, that from what I have heard on this floor, we are one people." [8]

Seven years later Moses E. Lard confidently affirmed:

"May we not boldly say, trusting in God to help us, we can never divide?" [9]

Others argued that division was impossible because with no organic union there could be no organic division. Joseph Franklin inquired how division could be effected and then responded:

"There is no ecclesiasticism to be divided." [10]

There seems to have been a reluctance to consider the possibility of division, and when the possibility was mentioned it was with the uneasy hope that it would never come about. As one examines the religous periodicals of the day he sees a group of Christians cascading toward the rapids of division, unwilling to consider their fate and even more helpless to do anything about it.

At the root of their plight was a deep doctrinal cleavage that had been three decades in the making. The societies and the introduction of instrumental music into an increasing number of churches were the most apparent indications of the condition. But the difficulties were there before the organ became an issue. There was an increasing awareness that the objective of union with the denominations could not be achieved without moderating the basic plea. Some were willing to sacrifice that plea, if necessary, to bring about union. Consequently, in spite of historic insistence upon immersion as a prerequisite to fellowship, we read of fraternal union meetings with the unimmersed.

The Central Church in St. Louis held several of these meetings in 1877, principally with the Congregationalists and Presbyterians.[11] When the church in East Cleveland dedicated its new $2000 organ in 1881 it invited a number of denominational preachers as participants. [12] Those who stood on the original platform erected by the Campbells began to feel that some desired peace at any price with the sectarian world. Congregations of the Reformation were increasingly viewed in denominational terms by their own members. One writer inquired why so many were leaving the Restoration Movement for the denominations and answered his own question by responding that the people had been taught so long that one church is as good as another that many didn't think it made a difference. The increasing abandonment of undenominational Christianity is clearly evident.

Coupled with these factors was a changed attitude toward the Scriptures in some quarters. German rationalism and theological liberalism became ideologies to be reckoned with in the Restoration Movement. Some clearly rejected the principle enunciated by Thomas Campbell that we must speak where the Scriptures speak and be silent where they are silent. Some of the avant-garde cried out against insistence upon immersion as a condition of salvation. The pastor system so completely eroded the authority of the elders in many places that in hundreds of congregations the organ was voted in over the protests of the bishops themselves.

The opponents of these innovations viewed these altered views and practices with alarm. What could be done to stop the tidal wave sweeping the churches? To resolutely oppose the changes would obviously jeopardize the unity of the movement and raise the possibility of eventual division. Yet to remain silent in the face of what they felt was a headlong rush toward apostasy would be to muffle their convictions and stand condemned before the Almighty. Some sadly subdued their consciences and in the interest of unity acquiesed in what was happening. Others determined to fight for their convictions. The ensuing battle ruptured a somewhat tenuous fellowship and precipitated eventual division. Plainly stated, the contention became so strong that continued fellowship was no longer possible. There is a relationship between harmony and fellowship. Break the harmony and you strain or sever the fellowship. No study of fellowship is complete unless it comes to grips with the way in which unity can be preserved in the face of what some feel are major departures from the truth.

Another factor that entered the picture in the division was conscience. For years the missionary society was an object of dispute in the Restoration Movement. Feelings ran high and bitterness was engendered. Yet the fact remains that the movement did not divide over this issue alone. A major reason was that while many opposed it, they were not personally compelled to accept it, and hence its existence did not cause them to violate their consciences. But when the organ began to be introduced, many faced a new problem. They felt it was sinful to worship with the instrument. When it would be introduced into a congregation over the objections of a minority, those who believed its use in worship to be wrong found their consciences offended by its presence. They could not worship in good faith where it was used. Under the circumstances, how should they react? In 1876 Benjamin Franklin counseled disciples in Charleston, Illinois, who felt they could not conscientiously worship with the congregation after the introduction of the organ:

"Declare non-fellowship with no one; say nothing about refusing fellowship, or leaving the church, or withdrawing from it. But deliberately and quietly meet in another place, and worship regularly according to the Scriptures . . . . Talk of no new church, 'second church,' or anything of the kind . . . .

"If the evil shall at any time be removed, there will then be nothing in the way of all meeting and worshiping together. If the evil shall never be removed, your way will be clear to go on and build up the kingdom of God in the community, set the congregation in order according to Scripture." [13]

Not all, however, recognized how conscience could be a problem. In 1881 one writer, in speaking about division over the organ in Bedford, Indiana, inquired, "How is it possible for anything neither commanded nor forbidden to be **in itself** considered a matter of **conscience**?" As he personally did not find the scriptures ruling upon the question he rejected the thought that use of the instrument could violate the conscience of another person. He overlooked the fact that the conscience is not governed by what is right or wrong, but by what one **thinks** is right or wrong. One may believe something to be wrong when it is not. Nevertheless, if he ignores his conscience he sins because he does not act from faith. "But he who has doubts is condemned, if he eats, because he does not act from faith; for whatever does not proceed from faith is sin" (Romans 14:23). Paul was discussing eating meats previously offered in sacrifice to idols. Because an idol is nothing, Paul reasoned that eating what is offered to it and then sold in the public marketplace is not wrong in itself (1 Corinthians 8:4-6). Yet, if one honestly believes such to be wrong and then engages in it, he is sinning because in violating his conscience he is not acting from the principle of faith.

This does not mean that one cannot sin if he always acts in agreement with conscience. Paul participated in good conscience in the stoning of Stephen and the persecution of the saints. Because of this he regarded himself as the foremost of sinners (1 Timothy 1:15). Only if the conscience is correctly educated by the word of God will it be an accurate spiritual guide.

The controversy over the missionary society seldom divided congregations. The organ controversy divided thousands. Brethren could worship together in spite of honest differences over the society. They could not worship as one if some insisted on using the instrument since this action violated the consciences of others.

The introduction of the instrument and the consequent division of many congregations did not immediately sever the fellowship of all in the Restoration Movement. Some opponents of the instrument felt there was still ground for a relationship. F. G. Allen, himself an opposer of the organ, quoted Isaac Errett with favor and added his own observations:

"Bro. Errett further says:

"'The law of love will not allow those who favor the organ to disregard the opinions of good brethren, or to make it the occasion of strife or division in the congregation; and the law of liberty will not allow those who oppose the organ to threaten division unless they can have their way about this matter.'

"To all of which we can say, Amen. The threatening of division does not enter into this controversy. We have planted ourselves firmly on this motto: we make nothing a test of fellowship that Christ has not made a condition of salvation." [14]

Allen failed to recognize that men in the heat of battle do not always act in accordance with the law of love. There remains a nagging question to which Allen did not address himself. If the law of love is violated and a minority is forced to leave by an offense to their consciences, is it still possible for fellowship in the true sense to exist? If brethren cannot worship together, do they really enjoy the mutual relationship implied in the term?

As churches divided over what some believed to be innovations, two distinct camps emerged. Those moving from one locality to another naturally gravitated toward those congregations with views approximating their own.

The alternatives facing those who felt that a major doctrinal defection was taking place were spelled out by John F. Rowe in 1883:

"If those who feel wronged and aggrieved withdraw from the Lord's people because of the presence of bad men who have brought in 'damnable heresies,' they not only surrender to the enemy, but they place themselves in a position which renders them powerless to remove existing evils and to produce a reformation. If, however, in their struggles at the post of duty and as faithful members in the one body, the true Israel of God are overpowered and the Church of Christ loses its apostolic identity by the presence of organized ecclesiasticism and priestly domination, in that case it will become necessary, according to the mandates of God quoted above, to actually separate and make a new rally upon the original ground. We have not yet reached that point and hope to avert the catastrophe if possible." [15]

A year later W. B. F. Treat asked, "Can we ever divide?" He responded:

"It is significant that the articles against division are written by the New Interest wing among the Disciples. They seem to fear that division will take place . . . . If there is any danger of division, it comes from 'the advanced wing,' the boasted 'progressive element' in the church. If they advance beyond the customs and practices of the first church, they will divide themselves from the true and the tried . . . .

"There is just one possibility of division among us, and that is for the progressive wing to persist in their present course . . . . The number and amount of things now being introduced bids fair to put those who are engaged in them, without warrant from God, where they can no longer claim to be the restorers of the church as it was in the beginning . . . . Of course, we could divide." [16]

It is apparent that the opponents of the "New Interest" group felt that a major apostasy was in the making, and if division did occur, it would be by virtue of that element departing from the apostolic position. Candor forces us to acknowledge that in any division the usual procedure is to place the onus for separation on the other party. However, Rowe and Treat made a valid point that there comes a time at which doctrinal error has so corrupted a group of Christians that they cease to be the church of God. Editors such as Isaac Errett of the **Christian Standard** and J. H. Garrison of the **Christian Evangelist** were hardly willing to acknowledge that this condition existed, but it is nevertheless a position that must be considered in any discussion of fellowship.

On August 8, 1889, a mass meeting of six thousand Christians was held in Shelby County, Illinois. During the assembly leaders of five area congregations issued a manifesto later called the **Sand Creek Address and Declaration.** Deploring what they considered to be departures from God's revealed word, they declared that if the innovators would not turn from their errors, they would henceforth no longer regard them as brethren. The churches represented did not purport to speak for other congregations. Yet their action was a recognition of the deterioration of relations among brethren within the Restoration Movement. Division was, at least in some sections, a reality. When the United States census report in 1906 listed the "Disciples of Christ" and "Churches of Christ" separately, it was but an acknowledgement of an existing breach. The plea for the people of God to unite had somehow floundered. As one looks back to discover what could have been done to maintain unity, he observes that given the attitudes and circumstances of the 1880's it is doubtful that division could have been avoided. The die had been cast twenty years before. While we cannot turn back time to recapture the unity of an earlier day, we can learn from the experience of the past as we seek to prevent further rupture of the divine family and strive to attain the blessed unity for which our Savior prayed.

By now it should be evident that glib generalities will not suffice in our search for true fellowship among Christians. It is not enough to quote John, "If we walk in the light, as he is in the light, we have fellowship with one another," and presume that we have a panacea for brotherhood discord. John's proposition is fundamental, but it does not address itself to our specific problems. We will, therefore, consider three areas requiring careful scrutiny. They are Christian liberty, heresy and false teaching, and the limitations of conscience.

The principle of Christian liberty was a foundation stone of the Restoration Movement. It was a basic tenet of Christianity much earlier. Many passages stress the freedom in Christ. Jesus taught, "You will know the truth, and the truth will make you **free**" (John 8:32). Paul wrote, "Now the Lord is the Spirit, and where the Spirit of the Lord is, there is **freedom**" (2 Corinthians

3:17). Again he declared, "For **freedom** Christ has set us **free**; stand fast therefore, and do not submit to a yoke of slavery" (Galatians 5:1).

Christian liberty implies freedom from sin and freedom from the law. It also means that each individual is personally responsible to God for his actions and opinions. "So each of us shall give account of himself to God" (Romans 14:12). In practice this means that no one can fetter the private convictions of a Christian. The early Restoration leaders tenaciously held to this cardinal principle as illustrated by the case of Aylette Raines. All agreed that Raines' opinions were erroneous, but he was still a brother, worthy of fellowship. Had Raines sought to impose his views on others there would have been a different attitude toward him. He had no more right to force his opinions on others than they did to compel him to reject his. The congregational member who militantly seeks to convert others to his opinions should be disciplined, not because of erroneous views, but because he is factious. "As for a man who is factious, after admonishing him once or twice, have nothing more to do with him, knowing that such a person is perverted and sinful; he is self-condemned" (Titus 3:10, 11). Unfortunately, Christians have frequently been disciplined, not because they were contentious, but because they personally subscribed to false teaching. While there is usually a factious element connected with false doctrines, it is unfortunate that the innocent disciple who shares an erroneous private opinion is often smeared with the same brush applied to the divider.

Reuel Lemmons has put the matter in correct perspective:

"Much of our trouble over fellowship has arisen because government in the congregation seeks to usurp individual freedom and impose the law of the government upon the private faith of the constituents. If individuals in a congregation surrender their faith to the government of the congregation, whether it be the elders, the preacher, or some strong-willed individual in the congregation, then they become slaves of men rather than slaves of Jesus Christ. Local church government may tell us what to do, but it cannot tell us what to believe. Only Jesus Christ can do that. It is true that one in a position of government in a local congregation may act as the Lord's messenger to tell us what to believe, and the Lord has arranged just such a communication system when he ordained that elders feed the flock. But their job is flock-feeding, not flock-herding. There are personal liberties we can surrender and there are personal liberties that we cannot surrender." [17]

There is great latitude in the family of God for differences of opinion. The New Testament clearly condemns certain immoral actions. Stealing, adultery, murder are sinful. But many things are governed by the application of principles involving human judgment. Our bodies must not be abused because they are the temple of the Holy Spirit (1 Corinthians 6:19, 20). But what constitutes abuse? Who can tell another how much he may eat before he becomes a glutton or that the drinking of coffee, but not tea, is a misuse of the temple of God? Christian women are to dress modestly (1 Timothy 2:9, 10), but how short may a skirt be before the principle is violated? These are individual decisions. Disagreement over them should never sever fellowship. On the other hand, the principles governing the decisions must become part of the thinking of each disciple of Jesus. Liberty is not license and must not be used as an excuse for wrongdoing. Peter enjoins us to "live as free men, yet without using your freedom as a pretext for evil" (1 Peter 2:16).

There is also room in the divine family for differences in doctrinal interpretation. We may disagree about whether a Christian may go to war. Yet the soldier and the conscientious objector worship side by side. Each makes his own decision based on his personal understanding of God's word. Why, then, have some issues disrupted fellowship while others have not? An example is the millennial controversy. For decades the nature and time of the return of Christ was discussed in the Restoration Movement without unity being impaired. However, about forty years ago a dispute about the thousand years of Revelation 20 caused a division. A major factor in the discord was the insistence of some that their personal interpretations of prophetic passages must be publicly pressed. In the controversy, however, lines were drawn not only against those **teaching** erroneous opinions, but also against those **believing** them and holding their views as private property. We need to inquire what makes one's belief in a millennial doctrine so much more vital than one's attitude toward engaging in military service. The drawing of lines of fellowship is often more the result of the temperature of a conflict and the personalities of the participants than the importance of the issue itself. It is time to reaffirm the right of private opinion. Let us be equally opposed to attempts to compel us to accept the opinions of others and to rob us of our own.

Any discussion of fellowship must eventually come to grips with heresy. False doctrine was the source of great difficulty in the early church. The circumcision controversy jeopardized the unity of the entire body. Later, gnosticism so threatened the purity of the Christian faith that John denounced its adherents as of the antichrist. "For many deceivers have gone out into the world, men who will not acknowledge the coming of Jesus Christ in the flesh; such a one is the deceiver and the antichrist" (2 John 7). He continued to warn against association with those who deny this vital element of truth.

Numerous sects appeared in the post-apostolic church in the second century, the most notable being the Montanists. Montanus, founder of the sect, was a Phrygian who proclaimed himself to be the **paraclete** or **Comforter** promised by Jesus (John 14:16, 25). Adopting a rigid asceticism, his followers were swept up in wild ecstasies. So severely did his teachings endanger the church that he was declared a heretic and his disciples became a distinct denomination separate from the main body of Christians.

We have already observed that fellowship is both vertical and horizontal. We sustain a vertical relationship with Christ, and because we are children of the same Father, a horizontal relationship with one another. Ideally, fellowship with God implies fellowship with one's brother.

Proceeding on this basis some have concluded that if another does not enjoy our fellowship, he cannot have fellowship with God. In other words, if we will not recognize him as a brother, God will not acknowledge him as a son, and he cannot be saved. This approach elevates man to the pedestal of judgment and arrogates to him the right of determining sonship. Sonship does not rest upon one's relationship to his brother, but upon his kinship to his Father. One is not dechristianized because of an imperfect relationship with his brethren.

Others have supposed that because of the relationship of each Christian with God there can be no legitimate barriers to fellowship among those born into the divine family. One editor states:

"We should make it clear that we make nothing a test of fellowship that God has not made a condition of salvation. Jesus declares that he who believes and is baptized shall be saved. If one can be saved from all the sins of his past on that basis, and is thus added to the one body, we ought not to demand more of him to be welcomed into our hearts." [18]

Thus, this writer concludes that if one is a child of God there can be no genuine barrier to fellowship with him. The vertical relationship requires the horizontal. It must be determined, however, what is meant by fellowship in this context. If recognition of sonship by other Christians is implied, the conclusion can generally be accepted as true. But, as already established, mere recognition that one has obeyed the gospel does not constitute fellowship in the biblical sense. How does false teaching fit into the picture? Did not John dictate withdrawal from Christian gnostics who denied that Jesus Christ had come in the flesh? Another writer, recognizing that there are some biblical restrictions on fellowship, acknowledges two bases for withdrawal:

"So far as I know, a brother is to be withdrawn from only for two possible reasons. If he deliberately and distinctly repudiates the confession that he once made of his belief in the deity of Jesus Christ, obviously he renounces the very basis of fellowship (2 John 7—10) . . . .

"The only other basis for withdrawing from a brother is if he denies the Lord by the way he lives." [19]

Denial of the deity of Christ and repudiation of him in personal living, then, constitute the sole reasons of separation. But this will not suffice. Should the post-apostolic church have allowed Montanism to go unchecked by blandly declaring that the heretical teachers were brothers because they did not denounce the deity of Jesus? What of modern day Joseph Smiths or Mary Baker Eddys who proclaim themselves prophets of God as Montanus called himself the Comforter?

Let us translate the issue into something all can understand. Suppose for a moment that we grant that Roman Catholics teach the truth regarding salvation from sin, and that on this basis they are part of the family of God. What, then, should be our attitude toward this institution and its members? Is there any possible way that the papacy and the hierarchy can be opposed without an absolute disruption of fellowship? Surely the Roman Church will not tolerate within its community those who repudiate so vital a doctrine. How can there be any semblance of fellowship when the errors of the mass, transubstantiation, and the confessional are exposed as errors? Christians cannot afford to remain silent in the face of such monstrous dogmas, yet to oppose them is to precipitate an intolerable situation in which fellowship in the biblical sense is impossible. Now, it may be reasoned that individuals enmeshed within such a system should be treated with respect and kindness and should be acknowledged as Christians by virtue of the new birth. But this is not true fellowship as there is no meaningful association in the scriptural sense.

"But," someone objects, "since the Catholics do not teach God's plan of redemption, we cannot enjoy fellowship with them in Christ." While this is true, it is not a response to the argument that there are vital matters other than a denial that Christ has come in the flesh precluding biblical fellowship. The Seventh Day Adventists supposedly teach that immersion is for the remission of sins. If we acknowledge that by virtue of a correct response to the gospel they have become Christians, can we conceive of a genuine relationship with them? They would be unwilling to worship on the first day of the week. We would oppose their sabbatarian views, the insistence on binding portions of the old law, and their recognition of Ellen G. White as a prophetess. This is too high a wall for fellowship to scale. To declare that we should make nothing a test of fellowship that God has not made a condition of salvation may sound fine, but it will not stand in the face of reality.

It should be emphasized that the reason fellowship with Catholics and Adventists is impossible (granting their obedience to the gospel) is not their private beliefs in transubstantiation or sabbath observance, but rather their promotion and practice of these views. One who believes he must worship on the seventh day is compelled by conviction to require that others do likewise. When they will not conform, he separates himself from their fellowship. The rupture is caused by his propagation of his error, not his holding it as a personal opinion.

On the other hand, is the presence of doctrinal error always grounds for withdrawal? If so, none of us would associate with the Corinthian church which Paul addressed as "the church of God which is at Corinth" (1 Corinthians 1:2). Not only were they factional (1 Corinthians 1:10-15), but they tolerated incest (1 Corinthians 5:1, 2), had brethren going to law with one another (1 Corinthians 6:1), had some who perverted the Lord's supper (1 Corinthians 11:17-22), and had others who denied the doctrine of the resurrection (1 Corinthians 15:12-14). Though Paul ordered the removal of the incestuous man, his antidote for the error about the resurrection was correct teaching. As in another circumstance he enjoined Christians to "mark them that are causing the divisions . . . and turn away from them" (Romans 16:17—A.S.V.), we may conclude that had the teachers of error persisted in promoting their doctrine Paul would have similarly advised. This remedy, however, was a last resort to be taken when ungodly leaven threatened the body (1 Corinthians 5:6-8).

As previously noted, Paul taught that the weak Christian should not be rejected because of disputes over opinions. "As for the man who is weak in faith, welcome him, but not for disputes over opinions" (Romans 14:1). The issues discussed are doctrinal— whether one might eat meat and the elevation of one day above another. If Christians may disagree upon such matters involving truth and error without a breach of fellowship, there must be other areas where we can disagree about God's word without separating. In fact, no two thinking disciples of Christ are in harmony on every doctrinal matter. Absolute conformity in biblical understanding would require a separate church for each of us!

An examination of Paul's stance in the circumcision controversy is helpful in putting false teaching and fellowship into perspective. The church did not divide over the issue at the time, although its unity was threatened. Later, the Ebionites, a remnant of the circumcision party, did completely separate from the church.

Paul's initial approach was to discuss it with the Judaizers and then with the apostles and other men of good will whose influence could be used to solve the difficulty (Acts 15:1—11). Paul refused to budge on matters of principle and declared, "To them we did not yield submission even for a moment, that the truth of the gospel might be preserved for you" (Galatians 2:5). He was willing to grant the Jews' right to their customs as witness his paying the charges of those taking the Nazarite vow (Acts 21:18-26), but he evidently did not feel that this act of accommodation compromised his stand against requiring the Gentiles to be circumcised. He warned the Galatians, "You are severed from Christ, you who would be justified by the law; you are fallen away from grace" (Galatians 5:4). Yet it is noteworthy that he did not refuse to associate with them. He proclaimed the truth without compromise, being as conciliatory as possible within the framework of that truth, but he did not take the initiative in severing fellowship. Division would come only when the Judaizers themselves drew lines of fellowship because of their unwillingness to work with the opposition. Paul was willing to retain fellowship with the circumcision party while he continued to teach the truth. Yet, tension created in such a controversy can cause separation, and we can be sure that had this occurred, Paul would not have compromised his stand for truth in the interest of unity.

A distinction must be made between the teacher of error and

the one innocently caught up in false doctrine. Passages in the epistles commanding withdrawal of fellowship relate to (1) the immoral and disorderly, and (2) the divider and false teacher. It is with the latter that we are here concerned. Consider these passages: "I appeal to you, brethren, to take note of those who create dissensions and difficulties, in opposition to the doctrine which you have been taught; avoid them" (Romans 16:17). "As for a man who is factious, after admonishing him once or twice, have nothing more to do with him, knowing that such a person is perverted and sinful; he is self-condemned" (Titus 3:10, 11). "By rejecting conscience, certain persons have made shipwreck of their faith, among them Hymenaeus and Alexander, whom I have delivered to Satan that they may learn not to blaspheme" (1 Timothy 1:19, 20). "Their talk will eat its way like gangrene. Among them are Hymenaeus and Philetus, who have swerved from the truth by holding that the resurrection is past already" (2 Timothy 2:17, 18).

These scriptures mark dividers and teachers of error as subjects of removal from the church. The stated reason is their adverse influence upon other disciples in preserving harmony and upholding the truth. However, the passages seem to apply to the teacher of error, not the disciple who passively accepts the false doctrine.

2 John 7—11 is worthy of special note in this connection: "For many deceivers have gone out into the world, men who will not acknowledge the coming of Jesus Christ in the flesh; such a one is the deceiver and the antichrist. Look to yourselves, that you may not lose what you have worked for, but may win a full reward. Any one who goes ahead and does not abide in the doctrine of Christ does not have God; he who abides in the doctrine has both the Father and the Son. If any one comes to you and does not bring this doctrine, do not receive him into the house or give him any greeting; for he who greets him shares his wicked work."

John clearly orders a rejection of the one who does not abide in the "doctrine of Christ," not even to receive him in one's own home. He has in mind the promoter of evil since he declares that the one "who greets him shares his wicked work." Bible scholars are divided over whether the "doctrine of Christ" is the doctrine **about** Christ (viz. that he had come in the flesh—verse 7), or the body of Chrisitan teaching taken as a whole. The original Greek allows either interpretation and the meaning must be determined by the context. The latter view would surely include the former as well. In any event, the passage states that false teachers should be opposed and rejected.

How should the doctrinal errorist be dealt with when he proposes his views among a group of Christians? Loyalty to Christ requires that he be opposed on the basis of God's word by those responsible for upholding the truth. Truth should be taught and error opposed, even though such action may severely strain fellowship with those accepting the error of the false teacher. The objective of this teaching should not be to drive these people from the fellowship, but should be corrective. Truth should not be suppressed out of fear that some might leave. This approach may necessitate marking the false teacher as a divider and disturber of the faith, and such an act may unfortunately cause some to hold to him for personal reasons rather than because of acceptance of his teaching. It is imperative in such action that those doing the marking keep "clean hands" so as to identify the source of the difficulty as the false teaching, not the personality. Eventually, either the correction will be made, or the disciples of the errorist will separate themselves from the body. If division results, those responsible for the false teaching will have caused it.

Summing up the problem of false teaching, it is evident that some doctrinal matters result in breaking fellowship while others do not. Our problem is to determine why certain factors make fellowship with others who have truly accepted Christ difficult, if not impossible. A correct response to the following questions will assist us in analyzing our difficulty:

(1) Does the false teaching subvert the basic message of the gospel? (i.e. a denial of the deity of Christ - 1 John 2:22).

(2) Does it threaten the unity of the body? If so, is it possible to oppose the error and still maintain a viable fellowship? Unity was threatened in the circumcision conflict, but the truth was still declared without causing overt division. It should be noted that error does not threaten our unity in Christ until it is promoted and practiced, unless it relates to a denial of Christ.

(3) Do those in error passively hold to their views or militantly promote them? Paul was longsuffering with the confused Christian enmeshed in error, but took the strongest stand against the militant agitator. "As for a man who is factious, after admonishing him once or twice, have nothing more to do with him" (Titus 3:10). Yet the mere holding of false teaching as private property without promoting or practicing it ought not to sever fellowship.

192

(4) Does the nature of the error cause another to violate his conscience if he is to enjoy fellowship in the sense of sharing? This will be considered next.

The conscience factor in the nineteenth century division of the Restoration Movement has been discussed. Conscience does not determine what is right or wrong, but it regulates actions growing out of what we believe is right or wrong. One cannot violate conscience and be right with God. Some controversial matters involve individual action in which the consciences of others are not affected. Neither the tobacco user nor the one who goes to war compels another by his behavior to smoke or enter the army. However, when Christians act in concert what one does may affect others. This is especially true in corporate worship. The brother who cannot drink the fruit of the vine from an individual cup may feel compelled to withdraw himself from a congregation using multiple containers. The same difficulty faces those who cannot in good conscience worship with an instrument of music.

In some cases there may be a solution to the problem when it arises within a congregation. One who sincerely opposes Bible classes might absent himself from this period of study without violating his convictions. A lot of people who have no convictions certainly do! If a Christian opposes using the money he contributes for a specific purpose there is sometimes a way of arranging the matter so that the objective is carried out without his specific donation being used for that to which he objects.

However, this approach is not always possible. We now face a very practical problem. If conscience prevents brethren from worshiping together, is true fellowship possible? In what more intimate way do we share than in worship? Granted, separate congregations are often found in the same community when doctrine is not a factor. Since they do not worship jointly some might conclude that they have no fellowship. However, it is often true that these churches will unite their forces on special occasions in a community of worship. When they feel the need to worship together there is no precluding barrier.

It was earlier suggested that there are different areas of fellowship based on the nature of sharing we enjoy. Christians do associate in ways other than worship. Can they have joint participation in such matters as work when doctrinal differences prevent mutual worship? Practically speaking it is extremely difficult. When doctrinal differences do exist, each church tends to reflect a specific viewpoint. If a congregation believes that a

193

doctrinal issue is sufficiently important to require worshiping apart from others, its members are unlikely to share their financial fellowship with an evangelist who may promote views with which they disagree. This type of situation arises in almost every area except the social, and if you cannot worship and work together, it is much more difficult to drink coffee together!

An unfortunate outgrowth of this situation is isolation which accentuates division. A few years ago fourteen meetings were held over a period of many months among Wisconsin and Minnesota preachers of the "instrumental" and "non-instrumental" persuasions. The meetings were designed to work toward unity on the basis of God's word. Never was compromise of convictions suggested. An amazing discovery was that mutual isolation of the two elements had often resulted in different terminology making communication more difficult. For example, to one group unscriptural meant what the Bible does not allow while the others used the term to describe what is in the realm of expediency.

After entreating the Father on behalf of the apostles, our Savior petitioned, "I do not pray for these only, but also for those who believe in me through their word, that they may all be one; even as thou, Father, art in me, and I in thee, that they also may be in us, so that the world may believe that thou hast sent me" (John 17:20, 21). Can we who acknowledge that all who have obeyed the gospel of Christ are a part of the undenominational church of God afford to ignore this divine prayer? Should we not take steps, faltering though they be, to work for the unity of the body of Christ? Surely those within the heritage of the Restoration Movement who still believe in the all-sufficiency of the scriptures can begin to seek rapprochment among themselves through meaningful conversations with the fulfillment of the prayer of Jesus as the goal.

Some oppose efforts to achieve unity on the ground that they will cause truth to be surrendered. That this has occurred in some instances is undoubtedly true. It does not have to be. Truth has nothing to fear by exposure to light. Two elements are necessary if dialog is to accomplish anything positive. First, there must be a commitment upon the part of all to the authority of the scriptures as the sole platform for unity. "Unity in diversity" will not succeed if by that statement is implied the abandonment of the New Testament as our means of achieving oneness. There is room among God's children for differing opinions, but essential truth can never be given up.

A second requirement of profitable discussion is an irenic spirit. One by-product of division is often a spirit of hostility toward those of opposing views. Militancy in labor—management negotiations may be a useful tool, but if expressed in efforts to bring Christians together it insures failure. There must be a willingness to acknowledge the basic integrity and good faith of "the others" and a commitment on the part of all to accept any truth exposed by God's word in the dialog. Even though one may be absolutely confident that on the issues being discussed he is right, God's truth, not victory, must always be foremost in his mind. May the Lord help us to be useful tools in achieving the unity of the spirit in the bond of peace, not instruments of Satan seeking to perpetuate division.

While this chapter has not discovered all of the answers to the problems of fellowship, we hope that it has placed them in better perspective. We ought not to fear renewed investigation of the theme, nor should we shun discussion with others who have obeyed the gospel, but with whom we have no meaningful sharing. The difficulties of division are extremely complex and do not lend themselves to simplistic solutions. While it is not too difficult to establish the basic principles of fellowship, the application to specific situations is often so involved as to challenge the wisdom of Solomon. It is imperative, of course, that all efforts to achieve unity be based on an honest search of the Word in an effort to determine the true will of the Lord. Compromise of truth will never produce genuine fellowship. One element which will go far toward the attainment of that fellowship requires no compromise—the display of a genuine attitude of **LOVE.**

## FOOTNOTES

1. A. S. Hayden, **Early History of the Disciples in the Western Reserve, Ohio** (Cincinnati: Chase and Hall, 1876), pp. 150-154.

2. **Ibid.,** pp. 167-169.

3. W. Carl Ketcherside, "Grilling the Editor," **Mission Messenger,** February, 1957, p. 3.

4. A. S. Hayden, **Op. Cit.,** p. 162.

5. **Ibid.,** pp. 163-169.

6. **Ibid.,** pp. 169, 170.

7. Charles Alexander Young, **Historical Documents Advocating Christian Union** (Chicago: Christian Century, 1904), pp. 75, 76.

8. James R. Wilburn, **The Hazzard of the Die** (Austin, Texas: Sweet, 1969), p. 195.

9. Moses E. Lard, "Can We Divide?" **Lard's Quarterly,** April, 1866, p. 336.

10. Joseph Franklin, "Union and Division," **American Christian Review,** January 31, 1884, p. 33.

11. News item, **The Christian,** January 25, 1877, p. 4.

12. John F. Rowe, "Organ Dedication at East Cleveland," **American Christian Review,** August 2, 1881, p. 242.

13. Joseph Franklin and J. A. Headington, **The Life and Times of Benjamin Franklin** (St. Louis: John Burns, 1879), pp. 413, 414.

14. F. G. Allen, **The Old Path Guide,** October, 1880, p. 384.

15. John F. Rowe, "Lift Up a Standard for the People," **American Christian Review,** September 18, 1883, p. 292.

16. W.B.F. Treat, "Can We Ever Divide?" **American Christian Review,** October 30, 1884, p. 349.

17. Reuel Lemmons, "More On the Key to Fellowship," **Firm Foundation,** September 17, 1974, p. 2.

18. W. Carl Ketcherside, "Searching for the Answer," **Mission Messenger,** January, 1960, p. 5.

19. Harold Key, "Basis for Disfellowship," **Mission Messenger,** April, 1963, p. 60.

# CHAPTER 14

# COMMUNICATING THE MESSAGE

"Is it true that you people think that only members of the church of Christ are going to heaven?" How often has this question been asked? That it has been asked at all is testimony to our ineffectiveness in communicating our plea. It is obvious that the religious world has not grasped the undenominational concept. There are two basic reasons. First, the religious community is not conditioned to accept the plea. Second, the idea has been poorly transmitted.

Consider the first factor. The great mass of society views Christianity denominationally. The average man thinks of the church of God as the sum total of Baptists, Catholics, Methodists, Lutherans, Presbyterians, and a host of other bodies, unless he believes his denomination is the true church and all others are apostate. To him most who profess to follow Christ are Christians and denominationalism is normal. It has not occurred to him that the early church was not splintered into sects. True, he may deplore division and wish denominations would get together, but his desire springs from a practical wish for greater harmony rather than from a longing to return to pristine Christianity. He believes that we are all going to heaven, but taking different routes. He has never seriously thought of the desirability of returning to the source of the stream and restoring the religion of Christ in its purity. He believes as he does because this is what his parents taught him and their parents before them.

This mind must be led to grasp a totally different philosophy. As he tries to understand it he may continue to relate Christianity to his former views. To transmit to him the undenominational plea will be difficult at best and impossible if care is not taken in the way the message is presented.

Next, better communication is necessary if the world is to appreciate the undenominational alternative·to the sectarian system. However, to establish how the plea can be better communicated, we must determine where we have failed in the past.

The first and most important reason that others have not understood the undenominational idea is that **those who seek to be just Christians have not comprehended it themselves.** You cannot communicate what is not clear in your own mind. Words with a sectarian ring proceed from a sectarian heart. It is unrealistic to expect our neighbors to understand us under these circumstances. To verbalize that one is undenominational and to think in non-sectarian terms are different matters. Words have a hollow sound unless the hearer knows that the speaker really means what he says.

To truly think undenominationally we must rid ourselves of the party concept. If one views Christ's body in terms of a "brotherhood" whose boundaries are defined by a set of personally determined loyalty tests, his understanding of the church will be thoroughly sectarian. Before he can adequately talk to others about being undenominational he must convince himself that God, not man, sets the limits of the kingdom.

A second cause of a misunderstood plea is **improper terminology.** If our words do not convey what we intend to say, there can be no true communication. For example, many books and pamphlets have been written on the theme, "Why I am a Member of the Church of Christ." They usually list identifying characteristics of the apostolic church and stress the importance of duplicating them today. While the writer may appreciate the undenominational plea, the title will prevent the average reader from grasping it. He has pre-determined that the "Church of Christ" is just another denomination. What he reads into the title is that the author is telling why his denomination is closer to the truth than others are. If the title were "Why I am Just a Christian," it would more effectively express the undenominational point of view without using language which the reader automatically construes as sectarian.

"But if we do that," it is objected, "others won't know what church we are a member of." Does this not say that we are trying to create a party image in the minds of others? We are unconsciously equating "our brotherhood" with the church of God as seen by the Lord. Unless we profess omniscience, we dare not say the two are identical.

Were a stranger to inquire what you are religiously, how would you respond? Would you say, "I am a member of the church of Christ" or would you declare, "I am a Christian"? Few would give the second reply which would more likely have been that of the apostles. Perhaps you say, "If I tell another that I am a Christian, he will then ask, 'What kind of Christian?' and I will have to reply, 'A member of the church of Christ.'" If this happens, why not say instead, "I am just a Christian, nothing more, nothing less; I am not a part of any denomination"? While some might think you presumptuous, you have at least opened the door to religious discussion in which you can explain the principle for which you stand.

M. C. Kurfees recognized the problem one has when he seeks to speak biblically:

"But it is further urged: 'If we simply say we are members of the church of God or body of Christ, the people will not understand us.' Why not? To be sure, they could not from such an answer locate one in any denomination; but this is precisely where one should not be located. 'But can we not say we are members of 'the Christian Church,' or 'the Church of the Disciples'?" Certainly, if that is the fact; but not if you wish to be undenominational and to speak where the Bible speaks." [1]

Another objection to using the simple language of the word of God is that some fear it will be offensive by implying that those in denominations are not Christians. Many years ago John S. Sweeney dealt with the objection in this way:

"Finally, we are told that our position unchristianizes all others but ourselves; that is, in accepting only New Testament names for ourselves and for our congregations, and in calling the body of Christ at large only by New Testament designations we dechristianize all who wear party names. We, however, fail to see the matter so. We dechristianize nobody. Does our professing to be Christian unchristianize anyone else? Surely not. Well, does our refusing to be or be called, anything else, unchristianize others? Certainly not. How, then, do we dechristianize all but ourselves? Does our wearing the Christian name logically imply that nobody else is a Christian? It certainly does not. As a matter of fact the disciples have ever held from the beginning of their effort to return to primitive Christianity, and do hold, that every Christian whether identified with any of the denominations or not, not only has the right to be, but ought to be, simply a Christian and to wear only New Testament names, as we ourselves are aiming to do."[2]

Words are vehicles of communication. It is not enough to argue that one is technically correct in calling himself a member of the church of Christ. If one understands "church of Christ" in a biblical sense this is accurate. But to the person steeped in denominationalism we communicate a different idea—a denomination known as the "Church of Christ." If the proper thought is not communicated we have failed in our objective.

A third reason undenominational Christianity is not understood is found in **misplaced emphasis** relating to the church. The message of the apostles to the world was that man is a sinner, Christ is his Savior, and when one accepts his Lord he will be added to the body of the saved. Contrast that with the frequently propounded theme that one must get into the church to be saved. That simply is not true because it makes the church the savior, not Christ. One is saved from his sins and in the process Christ adds him to His body. The church is the saved, not that which saves. It may be objected that Paul writes, "For by one Spirit we were all baptized into one body" (1 Corinthians 12:13). What Paul is declaring is not that the one body saves, but that by one's obedience he is added to that body. When some insist on saying "church of Christ members" instead of Christians it is usually an indication that the emphasis they have heard in teaching has been on church membership rather than salvation from sin.

A fourth factor contributing to a misunderstood plea is that of **improper attitudes**. Undoubtedly some who ask if only "church of Christ members" are going to be saved are motivated by prejudice. It is easier to launch an emotional appeal than to respond with Scripture when you cannot answer an argument. Yet, such prejudices have too often been created by a "holier than thou" attitude on the part of the one who professes to be just a Christian. No one likes to be assaulted intellectually. Most of us react negatively to a condescending attitude toward our knowledge. Even if we are convinced of the truth presented we reject it because we resent the approach. Therefore, in any religious discussion the Christian should acknowledge his fallibility and be honestly willing to accept any truth he is shown. If we expect others to hear us, we must be willing to hear them. But if we approach a controverted point with victory as the objective, we may whip our adversary in debate but we will not likely win him to our point of view. It is not enough to force a person into a corner and browbeat him until he confesses he is wrong. Even if he acknowledges the truth, he may react in bitterness because he sees an unchristian spirit displayed. How much better it is to suggest that differences should be discussed with truth as the objective. Each one agrees in advance to follow the direction of the word of God—and each one means it! Beginning with intellectual parity, the attaining of truth rather than victory becomes the goal.

We should be careful not to accuse another of refusing to accept the authority of the Bible because he rejects truth which we think is evident. All of us are sometimes hindered by mental blocks and he may be the victim of such. While it may be true that unwillingness to accept the Scriptures is the problem, it is more likely that prior teaching has created a blind spot which must be removed before the truth is apparent. When an honest person is informed that he doesn't believe the word of God because he rejects our conclusions, an irremovable prejudice may be formed.

Sometimes we may feel that another is rejecting the Bible when he is only refusing our interpretation of the Scriptures. It is easy to believe an explanation of a passage so strongly that any alternative exegesis is automatically rejected as renunciation of the authority of the Lord. Perhaps we have never even heard the other position fairly represented. In the history of the Restoration Movement there have been lengthy discussions of the means by which congregations can biblically cooperate. All who have examined the subject have gone to the same book to find the answers. Every explanation that has been given involves interpretation of God's word. To accuse any individual of rejecting the authority of Scripture because he does not accept a given interpretation is grossly unfair. It is much better to acknowledge that another still believes in the all-sufficiency of the word, even if we believe him honestly mistaken, than to accuse him of rejecting Christ because he cannot accept our explanation.

The dogmatic spirit has been responsible for more prejudice than anything else. It is far easier to create a prejudice than to remove it. Jesus admonishes us, "Be wise as serpents and

201

innocent as doves" (Matthew 10:16). The wise man is not dogmatic. It is not compromising the truth to tell another, "I will listen to what you have to say and examine your reasoning fairly in the light of God's word. I ask you to do the same with mine." The dogmatic individual is almost always deeply sectarian in his attitudes. We can see the characteristic in others; let us examine our own souls and remove any vestige of dogmatism we have not yet erased.

Having examined some of the reasons that undenominational Christianity is misunderstood, let us consider some positive suggestions for better communicating the ideal. First, it is important that we establish the need of being undenominational by showing the evils of sectarianism. Many people are already convinced that there ought to be a better way than is found in divided Christendom. The prayer of Jesus for unity in John 17 can do much to convince the Bible believer that religious division is wrong. Undenominational Christianity presents a valid alternative.

Next, since thoughts are transmitted by words, it is important to choose them carefully as we talk to others about our plea. The principle must be explicitly defined. Point out that the church described in the New Testament is composed of all the saved throughout the world as determined by the Lord, not man. Make it clear that when you refer to the church you speak of this body, not a denomination.

Third, if your friend has misconceptions, try to remove them. If he should inquire if you believe that "only members of the church of Christ are going to be saved," show that the church, by definition, **is** the saved just as a cocker spaniel is a dog and cannot be otherwise. Hence all of the saved are in the church. Be sure to establish that you refer to the blood-bought body of Christ rather than any sectarian organization. Once your listener realizes that you do not have a denominational concept, most of the confusion will disappear. If he responds, "That isn't the way one of your brethren explained it to me," kindly point out that you will not knowingly defend any erroneous position, regardless of who may hold it, but that we must all rather be concerned about what the Bible teaches.

Then, be willing to admit that no one's denomination will save anyone. Jesus is our Savior, not the church, let alone any human organization. As you do not believe that the Lord's body is a denomination, you have nothing to lose by making this concession and you may clarify a misunderstanding.

202

Be sure to speak as the oracles of God. In designating the church, refrain from the exclusive use of "church of Christ" or any other biblical phrase. Why not call the Lord's people the church of God, the Lord's church, or the body of Christ? Speak of those who proclaim the good news as gospel preachers rather than "church of Christ preachers." After all, it is the gospel, not the church of Christ, they are proclaiming. And instead of constantly referring to "church of Christ members," describe the saints as disciples or Christians as they are in the New Testament.

Next, in all things be humble. Some are inevitably offended by the gospel message, but be sure that the offense is not caused by the haughty way it is presented. A good maxim is to let your love shine through in everything.

Finally, refuse to be a judge. We are to preach the word, not to judge the lost. Many of us have encountered such queries as, "Do you think God will condemn the man on the desert who can't find enough water to be immersed?" or "Do you really believe God is going to send my dead mother to hell because she wasn't baptized?" These questions, though perhaps sincerely asked, are prejudicial. We are not called upon to pronounce judgment and we make a mistake when we do. Furthermore, by responding with a yes or no to such questions we feed the prejudices which are already there and defeat our efforts to teach the truth. How much better to reply, "God has not made me the judge and my opinion really isn't worth much. We know that the Lord will do what is right, whatever that may be. It is important for each of us to respond according to his knowledge of the truth. If we know the truth and do not accept it, we cannot expect mercy in the day of judgment."

There are millions of people who are looking for something in religion, but they do not know what. They are disenchanted by the empty formalism and institutionalism to which they have been exposed. Apostolic Christianity will satisfy their needs. When it is presented in an undenominational way, it has an appeal that cannot be matched when set forth in sectarian terms. It is up to those who believe in this message to share it with others who are hungering and thirsting after righteouness.

It would be difficult to improve upon the counsel of Paul in communicating the message: " . . . pray that I may proclaim it as clearly as I ought. Be tactful with those who are not Christians and be sure you make the best use of your time with them. Talk to them agreeably and with a flavour of wit, and try to fit your answers to the needs of each one" (Colossians 4:4-6, Jerusalem Bible).

## FOOTNOTES

1. M. C. Kurfees, "The Church Revealed in the Bible," F. D. Srygley, **Biographies and Sermons** (Nashville, Tennessee: privately published, 1898), p. 392.

2. John S. Sweeney, "Our Aim," **Sweeney's Sermons** (Nashville, Tennessee: Gospel Advocate, 1893), p. 146.

# CHAPTER 15
# THE SECTARIAN SPIRIT

They had been arguing about who was the greatest. Jesus gently chided the disciples by placing a child at His side as He said, "Whoever receives this child in my name receives me, and whoever receives me receives him who sent me; for he who is least among you all is the one who is great" (Luke 9:48).

How do you react when you are found guilty and have no reply? One way is to change the subject and this is what John did. "Master," he said, "we saw a man casting out demons in your name, and we forbade him, because he does not follow with us" (Luke 9:49). It is not difficult to note a jealous attitude toward the rival exorcist in John's statement. He does not seem to have been so concerned about the man's action as that he was not part of the "in-group" of the twelve. In fact, John's reason for forbidding him to cast out demons—"he does not follow with us"—betrays a party loyalty totally out of keeping with the attitude Jesus sought to instill within his followers. Jesus' response was to the point. "Do not forbid him; for he that is not against you is for you" (Luke 9:50). On another occasion He also taught, "He who is not with me is against me" (Luke 11:23). Combining the two declarations we conclude that we cannot be neutral respecting Christ. The exorcist was actually a follower of Jesus, but because he was not an intimate associate of the twelve John was unwilling to acknowledge him as a fellow disciple.

The sectarian spirit is the unseen foe of every child of God. Certainly John did not know he had a problem. The first century Pharisees pictured themselves as the staunchest defenders of the faith, yet Jesus verbally excoriated them for their sectarianism. "But woe to you, scribes and Pharisees, hypocrites! because you shut the kingdom of heaven against men; for you neither enter yourselves, nor allow those who would enter to go in. Woe to you, scribes and Pharisees, hypocrites! for you traverse sea and land to make a single proselyte, and when he becomes a proselyte, you make him twice as much a child of hell as yourselves" (Matthew 23:13, 15).

The Corinthians were plagued with partyism. Paul admonished them, "I appeal to you, brethren, by the name of our Lord Jesus Christ, that all of you agree and that there be no dissensions among you, but that you be united in the same mind and the same judgment. For it has been reported to me by Chloe's people that there is quarreling among you, my brethren. What I mean is that each one of you says, 'I belong to Paul,' or 'I belong to Apollos,' or 'I belong to Cephas,' or 'I belong to Christ.' Is Christ divided? Was Paul crucified for you? Or were you baptized in the name of Paul? I am thankful I baptized none of you except Crispus and Gaius; lest any one should say that you were baptized in my name" (1 Corinthians 1:10-15).

Because contemporary denominationalism is so deeply entrenched, our struggle against the sectarian spirit is even more difficult than in the time of the Corinthians. In its inception the Restoration Movement was viewed by its originators as calling men out of denominationalism into the simplicity of non-sectarian Christianity. They had not the slightest intention of founding another denomination, even one resting squarely on the apostolic pattern. They believed that thousands of Christians were enmeshed in denominational bodies. They called on them to leave "spiritual Babylon" and to find their fellowship among those disciples who strove to be **Christians only**. Although these men had not yet thought through all the implications of undenominational Christianity, they possessed a non-sectarian spirit that attracted hundreds of thousands seeking something better than the narrow attitudes they saw in their own parties.

However, when denominational doors were closed against them in the 1830's, the men of the Restoration faced a new dilemma. How could they maintain a separate existence as a religious body without at the same time partaking of the sectarianism which they condemned? Did their isolation from others imply denominationalism? Their problem was compounded by the large number of denominational converts who merely transferred their sectarian loyalty to the Restoration Movement. The increasing difficulty of maintaining an undenominational posture was rooted in the sectarian spirit of those who had never fully grasped how one could be just a Christian. It exhibited itself in various ways. The unbiblical terminology, the organizational struggles, the increasing traditionalism were but symptoms of an attitude from which all of these sprang.

When every aspect of sectarianism has been thoroughly examined, it is evident that **undenominational Christianity cannot be achieved apart from an unsectarian spirit**. Correct the heart and the language of Ashdod will disappear, the problems of fellowship will be diminished, and the plea for all men to be just Christians will be communicated with greater effectiveness.

In the last analysis, the attitude of the church is determined by the individual Christian. What is a congregation except an aggregate of individuals whose collective views mold its spiritual outlook? Change the individuals and you change the church. F. D. Srygley recognized this truth when he wrote:

"If there is ever a return to the unity of the apostolic days, it will be by individual action, and not by unanimous resolution. In New Testament times all Christians were but one body in Christ because no Christian belonged to anything but the body of Christ which is the church. All Christians belong to and constitute the body of Christ now, and no Christian has any divine authority to belong to anything else. Any Christian who belongs to anything but the body of Christ, which is the church, is in violation of the plain teaching of the New Testament, and his duty is to correct his error, repent of his transgression, and stand aloof from everything but the church, which is the body of Christ, and of which every Christian is a member." [1]

Since undenominational Christianity can be attained only through the development of the unsectarian spirit in the individual, discovering the nature of that spirit becomes imperative. Individual implementation of it becomes a sacred duty.

There are some attitudes which may be mistakenly construed as sectarianism. For example, a Christian is not sectarian in strictly adhering to the authority of God's word. Some feel that when another insists upon a "thus saith the Lord" for religious practices he betrays an intolerance incompatible with a true unsectarian spirit. It is argued that such a demand raises an unnecessary barrier against those who find their religious authority outside the Bible. It is true that some are unwilling to abide by the direction of the apostolic writings because they reject their divine inspiration. This alienates them from those who believe that the Scriptures are still the norm by which you must be spiritually guided. However, loyalty to Christ requires loyalty to His directives and those of His apostles. If such loyalty is a hindrance to union it must be so, but it does not thereby become an expression of sectarianism.

One is not sectarian because he stoutly opposes what he believes is false doctrine. True tolerance is not demonstrated in refusing to defend one's beliefs, but in possessing a proper attitude toward others and in a willingness to hear the other side fairly. Even if one is wrong in his opposition, this does not necessarily constitute sectarianism. Of course, it is often a short step from opposition to partyism. Much sectarianism is opposition gone to seed.

Nor does one become sectarian merely by calling for the removal of the denominational system. It is easy, of course, to become sectarian in opposing sectarianism. We do not improve matters by exchanging one brand of sectarianism for another as David Lipscomb observed:

"There are some in nonsectarian churches who are sectarians, who violate the laws of God in order to oppose sectarians. They are sectarians in their opposition to sectarians." [2]

The reader is now asked to consider whether any of several expressions of the sectarian spirit have personal application. To begin with, one demonstrates sectarianism in using sectarian speech. One's language may be biblical terminology applied in a sectarian manner. Using "church of Christ" to designate less than the whole body of our Lord (when not speaking congregationally) is symptomatic. To refer continually to "church of Christ members" rather than simply calling disciples of Jesus **Christians** betrays an infection of the disease. We must seek to eliminate the type of thinking that produces such speech.

Second, we betray a sectarian attitude when we display a party loyalty that is more concerned about defending the status quo among a group of disciples than in promoting the welfare of the entire church of God. The Christian lady referred to earlier who said she was "Church of Christ all the way" obviously had a loyalty to what she thought of as a party, but little loyalty to Christ Himself.

Party loyalty is apparent when we pride ourselves on being larger or more important than those of other faiths. In some ways it is fine when a church grows enough to move across the tracks from its old frame house of worship into a new air conditioned edifice with adequate classrooms and teaching facilities. Yet there is always a danger that its members will develop a pride that rejoices, not in the souls being saved, but in the respectability achieved by numbers and wealth. It is easy to rationalize that we are rejoicing for the Lord when we are only expressing party loyalty.

This kind of pride is evident when we bask in the reflected glory of others who share our religious views. Whether it be a sports figure, an entertainer, or a member of Congress, we are quick to tell others that "he is a member of our church." Perhaps it is God's providence that in recent years some well-known entertainment figures have proved embarrassing to those who had earlier lauded them. Such experiences should help us appreciate the values of Jesus who said, "Blessed are the meek, for they shall inherit the earth" (Matthew 5:5). True greatness is not achieved in knocking a home run or winning an academy award, or even in being elected president, but in truly becoming the servant of all.

James A. Garfield, twentieth President of the United States, was a gospel preacher in his early days. When he was elected president some brethren felt it imperative that they build a new house of worship in Washington to replace what the reporters sneeringly called the "Campbellite shanty." The old building just wasn't good enough for the President! A financial campaign was launched and in due time in the "Garfield Memorial Church" was built. But in reality the building was not so much a memorial to the President as an exhibition of partisan pride in having one of the same faith reach a position of such eminence. [3]

A third indication of a sectarian spirit is discernible in the one who equates a brotherhood of congregations with the church of Jesus Christ. To such a one the "brotherhood" is delineated by a correct name (such as **church of Christ**) and by a corresponding list of doctrinal issues upon which all must agree to be counted as part of this brotherhood. The issues change from time to time depending on the current controversy. Those who do not meet the test are not in the brotherhood and hence are outside the body of Christ.

To such a person "the church" is a specific group of congregations with which he is associated and of which he approves. He mentally excludes those churches in "doctrinal error" (as he defines error) as well as those churches of which he has no

209

personal knowledge. His conception of the church is too small to include all of the saved as determined by an omniscient Christ whose knowledge of human spiritual conditions far exceeds that of any human being.

Fourth, we express a sectarian spirit when we think we have a corner on the truth. Of course, few would put it exactly that way. Those of us who believe that the Scriptures are divinely inspired may simply affirm that we have the truth because we follow the Bible, and those who disagree do not have the truth because they do not follow God's word. Of course, it is correct to say that the Scriptures are God's revelation to man and that they constitute the truth. In that sense to have the Bible is to have the truth. Yet in the above reasoning there is the unstated assumption that "having the truth" is equivalent to interpreting it properly in every essential area. Candor forces us to acknowledge that others as honest as we also accept the Bible as God's word, and yet come out with different answers in vital areas. There is a difference between accepting the authority of the Scriptures and correctly interpreting it. It is the height of presumption and arrogance to assume that any group of people is exempt from the possibility of misinterpretation.

Who has not been repelled by the dogmatic assertions of the Jehovah's Witnesses who profess that they and they alone are infallible interpreters of the written word? Yet we can fall into the same trap. Some years ago I was one of three men asked to mediate some local church trouble. It didn't take us long to discover that much of the difficulty centered about the preacher who was unable to distinguish between the Bible and his personal interpretation of it. The issue was church discipline. While all agreed that it must be administered, some felt more patience needed to be exercised than the preacher was willing to allow. He therefore accused them of rejecting God's authority because they denied his application of the word. He thought he had a monopoly on the truth.

This attitude is seen in brotherhood watchdogs who exert political pressure against those suspected of deviating from the truth. They hit a "hard line" in religious papers and local church bulletins by exposing presumed departures from what is biblically sound. They attack personalities and reveal internal congregational difficulties to the detriment of those earnestly working to correct the problems. Facts are distorted to leave erroneous impressions. Like Diotrephes who loved to have the preeminence (3 John 9), these super-patriots of the Lord feed their own egos and establish themselves as defenders of the faith.

210

There are times, of course, when error must be publicly exposed. False doctrine cannot be allowed to win by default. But there is a vast difference between combatting error by God's word taught in the spirit of Christ and the rancorous approach used by those employing the search and destroy method.

Truth is the sole possession of no one. No man has a perfect understanding of God's will. We ought to be willing to accept any truth which others can give us. But to presume to claim private ownership of the truth is to be sectarian.

Finally, we exhibit a sectarian spirit in judgmental attitudes toward others. Men get into trouble when they try to do God's work for him. If we write human creeds as official interpretations of the Scriptures, we are legislating for the Lord. When we inform others that they are "going straight to hell" we are trying to do His judging. We have neither prerogative. The Christian's function is to teach the word and leave the judging to Christ. With our limited knowledge and understanding we are not equipped to pronounce judgment on anyone, and even if we were, it is not our responsibility.

In discussing a dispute about the body of Moses, Jude declares, "But when the archangel Michael, contending with the devil, disputed about the body of Moses, he did not presume to pronounce a reviling judgment upon him, but said, 'The Lord rebuke you'" (Jude 9). If God's archangel did not have the right to determine the destiny of Satan, who are we as God's creation to arbitrarily assign others to eternal punishment?

A reexamination of the subject of divine grace will help us to be less judgmental. Most of us appreciate the fact that God will forgive repeated moral sins, providing genuine repentance accompanies confession of wrong. We know that God will forgive His child who repeatedly loses his temper but consistently tries to overcome his weakness.

However, many do not realize that God also extends His grace to doctrinal matters. Some reason that when doctrinal error is persisted in there is no repentence displayed and without repentance there can be no forgiveness. This betrays a misconception of the nature of repentance. Repentance is a change of heart which says in effect, "Lord, I will change my life to conform to your will as I learn what that will is." One cannot repent of what he does not know to be wrong. A user of profanity cannot repent of his foul language until he is taught that it is sinful. Likewise, many honest people persist in doctrinal error because they have never learned that it is error. If they were convinced they were wrong, they would change. Who has the right to avow how far the Lord will or will not go in extending clemency to His children in either moral or doctrinal error? Paul inquires, "Who are you to pass judgment on the servant of another? It is before his own master that he stands or falls. And he will be upheld, for the Master is able to make him stand" (Romans 14:4).

In a sense it is true, of course, that the word of God judges men. If you read to a sinner the words of Jesus, "He who believes and is baptized will be saved; but he who does not believe will be condemned" (Mark 16:16), and if he rejects this teaching the Scriptures themselves have judged him. This is quite different, however, from our asserting that because a Christian ignorantly continues to err in a matter of doctrine he cannot be saved. When we display such a judgmental attitude toward others we have elevated ourselves into the judgment seat of Christ.

It is not too difficult to find sectarian attitudes in others. It is harder to see them in ourselves. The sectarian spirit exposes a deep-rooted malignancy which saps the spiritual vitality of those striving to be just Christians. It is essential that each one humbly recognize his own deficiences in combatting this malady. The battle must be waged at the personal level by each Christian overcoming improper attitudes expressed in speech and action.

## FOOTNOTES

1. F. D. Srygley, Editorial, **Gospel Advocate**, April 20, 1899, p. 241.

2. David Lipscomb, **Queries and Answers** (Cincinnati: F. L. Rowe, 1942), p. 381.

3. Earl Irvin West, **The Search for the Ancient Order** (Indianapolis, Indiana: Religious Book Service, 1950), Vol. 2, pp. 219-220.

# CHAPTER 16

# JUST CHRISTIANS

In its formative years the Restoration Movement experienced astounding numerical growth. So long as the religious world viewed it as a movement rather than a sect it attracted thousands of men and women who desired to be released from the shackles of ecclesiasticism. The plea for restoration of New Testament Christianity made sense to the common man who longed for the simple faith taught by Jesus. However, when the world came to view these people as the "Disciples denomination," this progress abated.

The early reformers laid down the basic principles by which men might return to the religion of the first century. Yet they knew they did not have all of the answers. They continued to redig the wells of truth in their effort to reproduce primitive Christianity. While truth is not variable, the conclusions of men searching for that truth must be subject to change as more light from God's word is discovered.

In any religious reformation there is a tendency to crystalize doctrinal positions. Thus Martin Luther's determinations were preserved for succeeding generations in his catechisms and confessions of faith. To this day these writings represent the norm against which his followers measure truth. While the restoration leaders steadfastly rejected all creeds, this did not prevent a certain amount of doctrinal crystalization. Generations which followed Stone and the Campbells were less concerned about a continuing search for truth and more occupied with

213

defending the conclusions previously reached. While defense of the truth is essential, we dare not slacken our effort to find still undiscovered biblical precepts.

There is a contemporary need to return to the searching attitude of the early Restoration Movement that successfully drew men from religious error into the light of New Testament Christianity. In the early nineteenth century many entire congregations embraced the restoration effort. They did not forsake all of their errors overnight. Step by step they were brought to a fuller understanding of the gospel. Restoration leaders exercised great patience with them in their transition from denominationalism to unsectarian Christianity. Today there are similar groups that can be brought to conform to the apostolic pattern with corresponding forbearance. An appeal to become part of the "Church of Christ" (which they view as another denomination) will not reach them. However, when non-sectarian Christianity is correctly presented, the apostolic appeal is compelling. But we who profess to be just Christians cannot effectively portray our message unless we first seek to close the practice gap by restoring those elements of our faith in which we are deficient. There are other wells of truth yet to be redug. Without the simultaneous restoration of these vital principles, the undenominational plea will be meaningless to others. The non-sectarian call is significant because it is an essential element of apostolic Christianity, not because it has merit apart from that faith.

We must redig the well of divine authority in spiritual matters. The Restoration Movement was rooted in a belief that a return to Christ required a return to His word. A dedication to the proper attitude toward the Scriptures is fundamental to the entire restoration concept. We must study the holy writ, not to defend pre-determined positions, but to learn the will of the Almighty. Then we must have the courage to apply what we have learned regardless of the consequences.

We must return to God-approved worship by restoring the divinely authorized elements of our devotional activities. Equally important, we must seek to worship in spirit, perceiving that worship is directed to God and is not just for the purpose of personal edification.

The restoration of the religion of Jesus requires us to go back to the personal commitment we find in the early church when disciples of Christ both lived and died for him. Christianity is not a Sunday hobby, but a vocation controlling every aspect of our lives. It is a way of life which demands that we give ourselves wholly to Jesus. Paul observed that the Macedonians had given liberally out of their deep poverty because they first "gave themselves to the Lord" (2 Corinthians 8:5). Such dedication requires us to give, not just what we possess, but of our very selves.

We must redig the well of Christian concern. "Bear one another's burdens, and so fulfill the law of Christ" (Galatians 6:2) is a fundamental maxim in a world that seldom cares. This teaching is rooted in the love of Christ from which flows our love for others. With it we aid our fellow Christians and reach out in compassion to the troubled human beings around us. As essential as doctrinal teaching is, the lost soul is more drawn to the Lord by the genuine concern of one who shares because he cares. Unless we show "God's love . . . poured into our hearts through the Holy Spirit which has been given to us" (Romans 5:5), our message will go unheeded.

Satan and his angels are hard at work filling in the wells of living water which Christ has dug for us. We fight a never-ending battle to remove the debris that keeps men from drinking of the unpolluted words of life. We dare not surrender our struggle on the basis that victory is impossible. Nor can we relax our vigilance, believing that the battle has been completely won. Truly, "we are not contending against flesh and blood, but against . . . the spiritual hosts of wickedness in the heavenly places" (Ephesians 6:12).

When the Restoration Movement began over one hundred fifty years ago the nineteenth-century reformers viewed restoration as a continuing process. As they discovered new truths they incorporated them into their teachings and practices. The concept of undenominational Christianity was developed and the implications of that ideal studied. But the encroachment of sectarianism was unrelenting, leading some to frankly espouse it and others to become contaminated by its influences. A practice gap between the ideal and the actual became evident. The gap is still with us and has discouraged many.

Yet, we should not despair. By the failures of the past we can better find our way into the future. Undenominational Christianity is a grand concept, beautiful in simplicity and difficult of execution. To those souls tired of the sectarianism of a divided world it has a compelling appeal that can exert a powerful force in bringing men to Christ. Still, it cannot be effectively disguised. Those who display partisan zeal while professing to be undenominational only repel the truthseeker.

215

As we encounter sectarianism in the body of Christ, let us patiently and persistently teach the truth. Much of the problem stems from lack of teaching. Jehovah instructed ancient Israel, "And these words which I command you this day shall be upon your heart; and you shall teach them diligently to your children, and shall talk of them when you sit in your house, and when you walk by the way, and when you lie down, and when you rise" (Deuteronomy 6:6, 7). Continual teaching is necessary to instill any principle, and if an older generation is unable to grasp this vital truth, we still have a responsibility to teach the young people who will be the leaders of tomorrow.

The failures of others are not a reason for us to fall short. One writer has observed:

"I have met brethren with a party spirit, just as I have met brethren with problems with alcohol. I have tried to correct and help both while approving neither. The party spirit of another does not make me a partisan. It is still possible for any individual to be just a Christian. It is also possible for many individuals who are just Christians to work and worship together according to the New Testament teaching and example. This does not make them a party or denomination. It makes them a church of Jesus Christ." [1]

Even though the quest for undenominational Christianity is admittedly difficult, it is obviously biblical and therefore not impossible to achieve. Those of us committed to it must first correct our own thinking and practice, and then, when we have grasped the non-sectarian plea, go and demonstrate to others that it is both possible and desirable to be **JUST CHRISTIANS**.

## FOOTNOTES

1. Cecil May, Jr., "Undenominational Christianity," **Firm Foundation,** June 10, 1969.

# SCRIPTURAL INDEX

218

# INDEX